Social Structure and Fertility Behaviour

Social Structure and Fertility Behaviour

Satish K. Sharma
Niranjna

Rawat Publications
Jaipur and New Delhi

ISBN 81-7033-658-9

Published by
Prem Rawat for *Rawat Publications*
Satyam Apartments, Sector 3, Jain Temple Road,
Jawahar Nagar, Jaipur 302 004 India
Phone: +91 141 651748 / 657006 Fax: +91 141 651748
e-mail: rawatbooks@pinkline.net

Delhi Office
G-4, 4832/24, Ansari Road, Daryaganj, New Delhi 110 002
Phone: 3263290

Typeset by Rawat Computers, Jaipur
Printed at Nice Printing Press, New Delhi

To
the
People of Kinnaur

Contents

Preface

The dearth of demographic studies in Himachal Pradesh in general and the tribal areas in particular drove us to explore the structural dimensions of human reproduction in the beautiful lands of Kinnaur. The special reason attracting us was that most of the studies conducted on the tribes all over India by sociologists and cultural anthropologists have, by and large, remained confined to the understanding of their ethnography, institutional dimensions----culture, marriage and family, economic and political organisation, etc. With regard to how the tribes perpetuate themselves over the generations and what kind of structural parameters operate in the process of human reproduction which constitute the fundamental basis of any community or the society, there exists very little knowledge.

Why do we need to analyse the demographic dimensions of a tribe? This is a very critical question which one needs to examine in the light of definite relationship that prevails between population and the developmental dimensions of a society. The range of relationship may vary from population as an essential and significant factor in the material development of a society to population as an impediment in the way of economic development. The underlying belief of the classical sociologists like Comte, Durkheim and the host of others was that under certain conditions the increasing population became a great source of labour force supply required in the production process (Boserup, 1965; Swamy, 1971). The other dimension propounded by Malthus and later followed by others suggested that increasing population adversely affected development process and the carrying capacity of the earth (Ravenstein, 1891). Even during 1950s, it was similarly argued by establishing a relationship between growing population and decline in the per capita cereal production. It is also well-known fact that the tribal areas for a considerably long time remained outside the purview of development processes and thus continued to be backward. It is, therefore, highly desirable to understand the population dynamics of the tribal area so that planners and the policy-makers are able to formulate appropriate development strategies.

The tribal people in India as a whole, in fact, have been the worst sufferers as the wealth of their lands have been exploited by the non-tribal population. Such a process of development, instead of fulfilling their needs, has resulted in their displacement from their own lands on the one hand and deterioration of their general social and economic conditions on the other. Roy (1993: 184-85) argues:

> "Even the land reforms and state operation of record of rights in the context of continuation of colonial legal epistemology of positivism, which sustains the theory of *resnullius* in contradiction to the age-old tradition of the country, can serve to divest the tribal communities of their rights over their land-rights having simultaneously economic as well as political or jurisdictional character. All this led to the marginalisation and pauperisation of the tribal people."

In the given conditions of the tribal people in general, the analysis of their demographic dimensions become all the more significant.

The present study, a modest attempt in the said direction, is the first outcome of authors' ongoing collaboration in the area of understanding demographic dimensions of a scheduled tribe in the north-west Himalayas. Methodologically, it is only through a systematic empirical observation of social life of the group or the community that one is able to find and understand differential patterns among what is observed (Babbie, 1992: 2). Further, elaboration of the observations becomes possible with the help of structuring of the research problem which involves exploration, description and explanation. What is being explored depends upon the relevance of the subject under study for the social order of the society, human groups and the individuals. The description refers to the elaboration of the situation or the phenomenon in a scientific manner with accuracy and precision. The explanation part pertains to the question of why a particular observed phenomenon prevails in a society as it has been observed. In this context, Babbie (1992:17) opines that there are two worlds of reality. First is the one which is known and called as 'experiential reality' and the second one is the 'agreed reality' about which one learns on the basis of empirical analysis of the situation concerned.

A systematic sociological study is guided by a research design, which basically refers to the planning of scientific enquiry. In other words, it elicits the strategy to find or explore a phenomenon. To specify what is being investigated and what is the best way of going about the research is significant in this process (cf. Babbie, 1991: 89). Since the present study primarily concerns with the structural dimensions of human reproduction, it follows both exploratory and descriptive methods.

Since human reproduction is also influenced by cultural system of the society concerned, the analysis focuses on the cultural setting of Kinnaur. The reason for placing the analysis in the cultural context being besides the socio-economic variables, the cultural factors have a determining effect. It is in view of this that it becomes important to look at the cultural aspects of women who give birth to the child, bring up the child and socialise him in accordance with the socio-cultural practices of the area. A total of 392 women were interviewed in and around village Sungra.

This work could be possible due to a grant of Rs. 15,000 granted by the Institute of Tribal Studies, Himachal Pradesh University, Shimla. Though quite meagre, this grant supported larger part of the fieldwork. It is here that more than financial support, the keen interest of Professor S.K. Gupta, the then Director of the institute and presently Vice Chancellor of the Himachal Pradesh University, Shimla, in this work helped us a great deal in completing the project. We, therefore, extend him thanks for his invaluable support to the project.

Thanks are also due to Miss Poonam Bhardwaj, Research Assistant, for the collection of data in the hills of Kinnaur. It was indeed the most difficult task which she accomplished well in time. She deserves our sincere appreciation.

Our friend Mr. Swaran Singh of Population Research Centre, Punjab University, Chandigarh helped us a great deal in processing the data. We thank him for extending us help and cooperation.

Satish K. Sharma
Niranjna

1 Introduction

Kinnaur, because of its strategic location and the defense needs of the country, has been receiving special attention of the politicians and the development-planners. Demographically also, it is the most populated among the scheduled tribe areas of Himachal Pradesh. In order to understand its peculiarity in terms of the relationship between its social structure and population dynamics, it is imperative to discuss the scheduled tribe areas of Himachal Pradesh. Methodologically, a comparative analysis of this kind helps in highlighting the special features of the area under study. It may be noted that the scheduled tribes in Himachal Pradesh constitute a minority in relation to the general (non-tribal) and scheduled castes population. However, due to their special constitutional status and the provision for their reserved electoral constituencies, they have become an important category for sociological analyses. This chapter, therefore, focuses on the following points:

1. The scheduled areas, their constitutional and geographical dimensions in Himachal Pradesh with special reference to Kinnaur;

2. Socio-cultural profile and spatial concentration of Kinnaura population; and
3. Patterns of population growth with special reference to fertility patterns in Kinnaur.

The Scheduled Areas: Their Constitutional and Geographical Dimensions

It is well known that the contemporary tribal areas and their inhabitants have been an integral part of Himachal Pradesh since long. An order of the Government of India, promulgating these areas and the people as the scheduled areas and the scheduled tribes respectively, came much after the inception of the state. It was on November 21, 1975, after a lapse of 27 years that Fakhruddin Ali Ahmed, the then President of India, passed an order and declared:

1. "(i) This order may be called the Scheduled Areas (Himachal Pradesh) Order, 1975.
   (ii) It shall come into force at once.
2. The areas in the state of Himachal Pradesh specified below are hereby declared to be the scheduled areas within the state:
   (i) Lahaul and Spiti district;
   (ii) Kinnaur district;
   (iii) Pangi tehsil and Bharmaur sub-tehsil in Chamba district.
3. Any reference in the preceding paragraph to a territorial division, by whatever name indicated, shall be construed as a reference to the territorial division of that name existing at the commencement of this order" (*Compendium*, 1993: 3).

Following this order, two complete districts, namely, Lahaul and Spiti, Kinnaur and parts of third district Chamba, i.e., Pangi tehsil and Bharmaur sub-tehsil became scheduled tribes areas covering 23,655 sq km territory which accounts for 42.49 per cent of the total geographical area of the state.

> Lahaul and Spiti, located between 31 41' 57" and 32 59' 57" north latitudes and between 76 46' 29" and 78 41' 34" east longitudes, is bordered by Tibet in the east, Ladakh in the north, Chamba in the west and Kullu in the south. The most distinguishing feature of this district is that it comprises two different mountain tracts---as is obvious from the nomenclature---Lahaul and Spiti. Another notable dimension of this district is the territorial jurisdiction running into 13,835 km which forms almost 57 per cent of the total tribal area and 24.85 per cent of the total geographic area of the state. Contrary to the large size of the district, its population is very sparse.

The entire district is rural. There are 239 inhabited villages. The tehsil-wise distribution evinces 65 villages in Udaipur sub-tehsil, 127 in Lahaul and 47 in Spiti. The total number of households is around 6,446 out of which 6,374 constitute occupied residential households. It is also worthwhile to note that both Lahaul and Spiti have been parts of different kingdoms till 1846----the time when the British established their control over these areas. Lahaul was a part of Ladakh kingdom till mid-seventeenth century. Afterwards, it was ruled by Kullu Chief. It was in 1941 that Lahaul and Spiti became a separate sub-tehsil. This was a historical event during which the local Thakurs were divested of their powers and the administration of the sub-tehsil was taken over by the state administration. In 1960, Lahaul and Spiti were merged and made a district of Punjab. Spiti was made its sub-division (Punjab Government, 1960).

Both Lahaul and Spiti constitute two different physical entities from within as well as outside. Their topographical location indicates that Lahaul constitutes the western and physically more accessible terrain in comparison to Spiti. The latter, being more difficult terrain, both in terms of climatic conditions and habitation, is relatively less developed in comparison to Lahaul. In fact, Spiti constitutes typical mountain desert with very little and sparse vegetation.

The district Kinnaur, a secluded and rugged mountainous region, is located between 30° 04' 50" and 32° 05' 15" north latitudes and between 70° 00' 45" and 70° 00' 35" east longitudes. Like Lahaul and Spiti, the entire district is rural. Not even a single individual had returned himself as urban till the conductance of the last census in 1991. Spread over 6,401 sq km and occupying 11.50 per cent of the state territory, Kinnaur represents unique physical and cultural region. On its eastern side lies western Tibet and on the south it touches Uttarkashi region of Uttar Pradesh and Rohru tehsil of Shimla district. On its north and west, it adjoins Spiti sub-division of Lahaul and Spiti district and Rampur tehsil of Shimla district. The maximum area of the district has remained uninhabited due to vast snow-covered mountains, inaccessible terrain and thick forests. The extremely cold climatic conditions, to a significant extent, have influenced the lifestyle and chances of the people survival.

The district is divided into three sub-divisions, namely, Nichar, Kalpa and Pooh. While Nichar constitutes the only tehsil of the subdivision, Kalpa and Pooh have two tehsils each, namely, Kalpa and Sangla and Pooh and Moorang respectively. Pooh has one sub-tehsil called Hangrang. Kinnaur has 12,457 households of which 12,299 constitute occupied residential houses (Census, 1981). In all, there are 77 inhabited villages. Their further divisions indicate eight villages in Hangrang sub-tehsil, 12 in Pooh, 12 in Morang, 12 in Kalpa, 22 in Nichar and 11 in Sangla. On an average, each village has 161.77 households and 159.72 occupied residential households.

Historically, Kinnaur existed as a tehsil of the Bushahar princely state. It was in 1960 that due to administrative prerequisites involving efficiency and convenience it was declared as an independent district of Himachal Pradesh. Like other mountainous regions, the living conditions in this part are also very tough. Some of its parts, especially the ones above 5,200 m from the average sea level, are under permanent snow. In other parts of Kinnaur district, some areas remain snow-covered for almost six months in a year. The lower regions, falling between 1,200 and 2,000 m above the sea level, receive snow only during the winter season. Accordingly, the human habitation is influenced greatly by the differential climatic conditions prevailing in the region.

Pangi tehsil and Bharmaur sub-tehsil, the two parts of Chamba district, are the other scheduled areas. These are spread over 3,178 sq km which form 6.49 per cent of total land area of Himachal Pradesh. Historically, Chamba existed as a princely state. The geographical location of Chamba is between 76° 30' 77" north latitude and 33° 00' 30" east longitude. Its southern boundaries share a common border with Kangra district of Himachal Pradesh. To its north lie Jammu and Kashmir. On the eastern side, Chamba touches Lahaul-Spiti and parts of Kangra district. On the Western front, it adjoins parts of Jammu & Kashmir state. The entire district is divided into five subdivisions, namely, Chamba, Churah, Pangi, Bharmaur and Dalhousie. It has five tehsils, namely, Chamba, Churah, Pangi, Bharmaur and Bhattiyat and three sub-tehsils namely Salooni, Holi and Shiunta.

The tribal areas of Chamba, viz., Pangi and Bharmaur, have

60 and 104 inhabited villages respectively. In comparative terms, Bharmaur sub-tehsil occupies more territory than Pangi. These two parts were promulgated as tribal areas on the criterion of 50 per cent concentration of tribal population. At present, the tribal population in these two parts is about 61 per cent of their total population (Census, 1991).

Table 1.1

Scheduled Area Population (1991)

District	*Population*		*Total*	*Density of Population*	*Sex Ratio*
	Males	*Females*			
Kinnaur					
Kinnaur	38,394 (25.35)	32,876 (21.70)	71,270 (47.05)	11	856
Lahaul-Spiti					
Lahaul	11,796 (7.78)	9,907 (6.54)	21,703 (14.33)	3	840
Spiti	5,428 (3.58)	4,163 (2.74)	9,591 (6.33)	1	767
Chamba					
Pangi	7,722 (5.09)	7,238 (4.77)	14,960 (9.88)	9	937
Bharmour	17,717 (11.69)	16,192 (10.69)	33,909 (22.38)	19	914
Total	81.057 (53.52)	70,376 (46.46)	1,51,433 (100.00)	6	868
Himachal Pradesh	26,17,467 (50.62)	25,53,420 (49.38)	51,70,877 (100.00)	92	976

Note: Figures in parentheses indicate percentages worked out of total population of the scheduled tribe areas.

Source: Tribal Sub-Plan 1992-97 and Annual Plan 1993-94, p.4.

The all the scheduled areas are situated in the north and north-east of Himachal Pradesh. They form a continuous belt in the far hinterland behind high mountain passes. Location-wise, these areas fall in the remotest and inaccessible region of the state. Although there are inter-area and intra-area variations in the altitude, yet on an average, each tribal region lies at the height of 3,281 m above the mean sea level. The distribution of population in scheduled areas is shown in Table 1.1.

Table 1.1 shows scheduled area-wise distribution of population. The table reveals that the scheduled areas of Lahaul and Spiti have 21,703 (14.33%) and 9,591 (6.33%) population respectively. Their male population constitutes 7.78 per cent and 3.58 per cent respectively and the female population is 6.54 per cent and 2.74 per cent respectively of the total population of the tribal areas. The total number of persons in Pangi and Bharmaur is 14,960 (9.88%; 5.09% males and 4.77% females) and 33,909 (22.38%; 11.69% males and 10.69% females respectively). The sex-ratio is the highest in Pangi and the lowest in Spiti scheduled areas. This is perhaps due to negative rate of growth of population in these two areas. Amazingly, Spiti's population growth during 1981-91 decade has been -7.44. The same trend continues even in 2001. Pangi has the highest rate of population growth (22.06) which even surpasses the 20.79 per cent growth rate of the state as a whole. The density of population is the lowest (just 1) in Spiti and maximum (19) in Bharmaur.

It may also be of relevance, especially from the viewpoint of population growth, development planning and policy formulation, that the scheduled areas contain only 48 per cent of the total scheduled tribes population of the state. However, 69 per cent of the total population of the scheduled areas falls under scheduled tribes category, 18 per cent under scheduled castes and remaining 13 per cent under other categories. At this point, it is also imperative to point out that among the tribals, caste distinctions remain significant and the scheduled castes also constitute part of the tribal population (TSP, 1993: 4-5). According to the 1991 census, districts Bilaspur, Kangra, Kullu, Shimla, Mandi, Solan, Sirmaur, Hamirpur, and Una districts have nearly 3.34, 0.10, 3.75, 1.86, 4.06, 0.87, 2.50, 0.02, and 0.01 per cent respectively of their total population as the scheduled tribes population respectively.

The Scheduled Tribes: Socio-cultural and Spatial Profile

Like the scheduled areas, the scheduled tribes are characterised by extreme heterogeneity caused by variations in their nomenclature, region of concentration, occupational callings, customs, traditions, lifestyle and so on (cf. Bajpai, 1987; Chib, 1984; Shashi, 1977; Negi, 1976). According to the constitutional and administrative criteria, there are eight scheduled tribes, viz., Bhot or Bhod, Gaddi, Gujjar, Jad or Lamba or Khampa, Kinnaura or Kannaura, Lahaula, Pangwala and Swangla.

The population of these tribes varies considerably from each other. Table 1.2 indicates that Gaddis constitute maximum number of the tribals followed by Kinnaura, Gujjar and Bhot. In comparison to these, the remaining tribes have very less to negligible representation. This is also true in relation to the total population of the scheduled tribes in the state. The Jad or Khampa or Lamba have a marginal share in terms of their number. The same is true of Lahaula. The population of Pangwals and Swanglas is more than Lambas and Lahaulas. They, as a separate ethnic, form a visible minority in relation to significantly visible majority ethnics, namely, Gaddi, Kannaura and Gujjar. The Lahaulas and Khampas, due to their very small numerical strength, constitute invisible ethnic minorities in relation to all. In view of their numerical strength, the scheduled tribes of Himachal Pradesh can be grouped into three

Table 1.2

Scheduled Tribe Population of Himachal Pradesh

Scheduled Tribe	*Population*		*Percentage to Total ST Population*	
	Male	*Female*	*Male*	*Female*
Gaddi*	38,937	37,923	39.04	38.87
Kinnaura	23380	24,533	23.44	25.15
Gujjar*	14,707	13,414	14.74	13.75
Bhot or Bhod	11,333	11,302	11.36	11.58
Pangwala	5,688	5,514	5.70	5.65
Swangla	3,663	3,499	3.67	3.58
Lahaula	1,021	853	1.02	0.87
Jad, Lamba, Khampa	753	460	0.75	0.47
Total	99,727	97,536	99.73	99.92

*Excludes those living in the territories specified under Subsection (1) of Section 5 of the Punjab Reorganisation Act 1966.

Source: Census of India 1981, Series 7, Himachal Pradesh Special Tables for scheduled tribes.

major categories. First, a significantly visible majority comprising Gaddis and Kannauras; second, a visible minority comprising Gujjars and Bhods; and the third, invisible minority formed by Jad or Khampa or Lamba, Lahaula, Pangwala and Swangla. Sex-wise males in general have more representation than the females, except for the case of Kinnauras. Two demographic characteristics, conspicuous in the census data, emerge dominant. Firstly, there exists a socio-demographic structure of scheduled tribes in Himachal Pradesh which consists of the majority and visible and invisible minority. The demographic hierarchy of the state represents these tribes in a hierarchical system in which these groups are placed in a descending order. This implies that the numerical position of a tribe corresponds to the relative position it has in the power structure of the state. It may be mentioned here that Kinnauras are not only a demographic majority among tribes but also the members of this group occupy positions in state administration which command relatively more respect and prestige in relation to others. But Gaddis who represent the maximum number among the scheduled tribes do not have a position similar to Kinnauras because of their nomadic life in the past. This comparative picture of the Kinnauras and Gaddis also suggests that to be a majority the number alone does not matter. Along with number, the group also needs to have material possessions and positions of some power and authority. It is because of their relatively better off social and economic positions, the Kinnauras are, perhaps, placed on the top of the hierarchy of the tribes in Himachal Pradesh.

The second significant aspect to mention is that the overall sex-ratio at present in Kinnaur is 856 females to 1,000 males. This sex-ratio includes the tribal and the non-tribal population. However, when one looks at sex-ratio of Kinnauras alone the number of females among them is more than that of the males. When examined in the inter-tribal context, the sex-ratio considerably differs from each other.

Besides the numerical variations, the scheduled tribes also represent socio-culturally distinct categories. These differences are conditioned by the historical as well as geographical conditions of their respective habitats. The Gaddis, who are numerically preponderant, are believed to have their place of origin elsewhere than Chamba. Their preponderance in Bharmaur, in particular, has been due to the invasions in plains and consequent immigrations of the defeated to the hills. Hutchison and Vogel (1982: 273) observe:

> "The Gaddi Brahmans have a tradition that their ancestors came from Delhi around 780-800 A.D. Many of the Rajputs (among

Gaddis) are probably the descendants of invaders from plains. The Gaddi Rajputs have the same tradition as the Gaddi Brahmans as to their original home: while the Gaddi Khatris say that their ancestors fled from Lahore to escape persecution, probably at the time of the early Mohammedan invasion."

Historically, the Gaddis form a separate clan. Being a generic group, they include Brahmans, Rajputs, Khatris and Rathis. In other words, they carried their social structure with them and the same continues in the form of caste stratification. The occupational heritage of the Gaddis indicates that they have been a semi-nomadic, semi-pastoral and semi-agricultural group. This fact of the Gaddis' history, thus, provides enough evidence to suggest that not all of them have been nomads. Some of them did lead a settled life as agriculturists. Their occupational callings also conform this historical fact as the above mentioned occupations are related to each other and this type of division must have been the outcome of the consciously designed occupational system among them.

In fact, traditionally, they have been the inhabitants of Bharmaur *Wazarat* (principality) called *Gadaran*. The term "*Gadaran*" is derived from Sanskrit word *Gadar* which means "a sheep". *Gadaran*, therefore meant "country of sheep" and *Gaddi* meant "a shepherd" (Hutchison and Vogel, 1982: 274). Therefore, the combination of the two refers to constant movement of Gaddis from their somewhat permanent place of residence to their temporary homes. This remains the feature of Gaddi lifestyle even in contemporary times. Some of the Gaddis keep on shuttling between high and low hills and the valleys during summers and winters respectively. This is a must for them as they have to go out along with the herds of their cattle in search of grazing fields. Despite their moving homes, one thing remains unique about them, i.e., they have preserved their joint family system even in the present times. It is not clearly known as to what extent this institution has survived but according to some casual observations they have been able to preserve this system till today.

The religious beliefs, festivals and worship practices remain quite strong among the Gaddis. *Nawala* (a special prayer) is the most favourite festival of Gaddis of Chamba. Lord Shiva is the highest god worshipped by them. They always invoke him in the times of distress as well as at the time of performing of certain type of, what Durkheim terms as the sacred and the mundane actions (social, economic or otherwise). The religious tradition enjoins upon almost each and every member of the Gaddi household to perform *Nawala* once in his life-time. Lord Shiva, as is believed, is invoked on almost all important occasions including marriage ceremony, construction of a new house, house-warming ceremony, etc.

Another socio-cultural aspect of Gaddis refers to caste hierarchy among them. Although it is difficult to argue on the rigidity of the caste structure and the nature of distinctions, yet in view of the nomenclatures assigned to people, such as Brahman, Rajput, etc., the caste structure seems to operate on the same lines as in the case of Hindu society at large. These distinctions suggest some type of functional divisions in the Gaddi community for the performance of varied tasks on the one hand and generation of a socio-economic hierarchy representing unequal power relations among them on the other. Although there exists differentiation as the mode of distinctions, yet the presence of a hierarchical system is another important dimension emerging among them.

The Kinnaura or Kannaura, the subject of the present study, constitutes the second largest tribe of Himachal Pradesh. The general belief about its origin describes them as the descendant of mythical Kinner, a distinct race, who are neither a human being nor god but a combination of the two or falling somewhere between the two. According to description of a Kinner, it represents human body mounted upon by the head of a horse or vice versa. Mythological belief is that such people are super human beings. Such formulations, however, lack empirical evidence and therefore, depict the tribe having mystical origin. The historians tend to differ from such explanations and propound the view that Kinnauras, though at one time pastoral people, have their origin in Tibet. Their settlement in Kinnaur dates back to ninth and tenth centuries when they were forced to abandon their place of origin.

Originally a polyandrous tribe, the Kinnauras have been living in joint families for centuries. Even in contemporary times, the members of same descent (such as father, sons, brothers, uncles, etc.) can be found living under the same roof with common ownership of property. At the same time, the evidence of nuclearisation of family is also in vogue. Even in some such cases the property remains undivided. The inheritance of property among them is governed by patriarchal system. Unlike tribal areas, the property belongs to families and individuals and not the tribe as a whole. This is suggestive of the fact that among Kinnauras, the individualism has been there which encouraged private ownership of property. However, the major significance of polyandry for Kinnauras has been the integration of the family as a unit and prevention of fragmentation of family landholdings and other property for quite sometime. Besides its functional importance, the dysfunctional aspect of such a practice had been there. The major one was the exploitation of women by their menfolk. Although women are described as industrious and very vital in the household and agricultural operations, yet the fact remains that due to patriarchy they continue to be dependent upon men for their survival.

Even today, the empirical reality is not much different from the one existed decades ago as far as women's socio-economic status is concerned. In the context of demographic dimension, the status of women and the nature of their work involvement constitute significant aspects of analysis.

Like most of the people living in hills, the Kinnauras are quite religious and superstitious. They believe in ghosts, spirits of the deads, and supernatural beings. Every village has its own *devta* (deity) whom they worship and attach very high value. About the superstitious nature of the people and the kind of practices they carry out Mamgain (1971: 84-85) writes:

> "People attach somewhat of a sacred and mysterious virtue to horns of domestic animals... the tops of hills are virtually sacred to Kali (Goddess)... importance is attached to dreams. To eat food or kill a tiger in a dream means success at work."

The Kinnauras are mostly god fearing people. However, as persons, as the historical observations suggest, they are brave, fearless, simple and straightforward people. Describing them people of good integrity, Gerard (1841) observed that they were the frankest and the most honest race of people... They possessed neither craft nor ingratitude and they were trusted to the world's end. In more than one way, they were believed to have remained unaffected by the ongoing changes in the society at large as late as 1940s. Johri (1964) cited and Mamgain (1971) referred to the continuation of some of their age-old practices as an indication of the limited change in the Kinnaura society. The practice of human sacrifice as late as 1940s is significant to uphold the said viewpoint.

Like Gaddis, the Kinnauras, too, do have a social structure of their own with hierarchical divisions within. This is quite evident from the terms used for their identification such as

"*Khashia*" (non-scheduled castes) and "*Beru*" (scheduled castes) on the one hand and the restrictions on marriages between the two groups on the other. Mamgain (1971:76-77) refers to social stratification and practice of restrictions in commensal and connubial relationships in the Kinnaur tribe. The status consciousness seems to determine inter-caste relationships among the Kinnauras too. The term "Kinnaura", like Gaddis is also generic and therefore, includes different castes within its fold. These are Brahmin, Kshatriya, Rajput, low castes like Chamars, etc.

Their occupational structure in the contemporary times represents cultivators, workers in household industry, construction and other industrial occupations, by virtue of which the Kinnauras not only have segmental divisions in terms of caste but they are also characterised by occupational differentiation. Their increasing educational mobility, entry into bureaucracy and technocracy have also set in motion the process of class formation among them. The kinship and family ties are quite strong and preserved significantly. The impact of socio-economic development is conspicuous in their emerging social, economic and political substructures and behaviour patterns. The latter refers to the visible consciousness about their rights.

The Gujjars, comprising the third largest scheduled tribe of Himachal Pradesh, like Gaddis have been pastoral and nomadic people, wandering from place to place in search of green pastures for their livestock. Spread all over Himachal Pradesh, excepting Kinnaur and Lahaul and Spiti districts, they are basically Mohammedans. Negi (1972:145) described Gujjars as entirely dependent on their herds of cattle. They are not a settled community as yet. Although the government has been spending money for their settlement, the efforts have not borne fruit. In some cases, though stray, the Gujjars have been found to be undergoing social change as a result of the acquisition of landed property and construction of permanent houses. The Gujjar economy has gained appreciable momentum as a consequence of the growing market economy and enhanced price of milk and milk products. They, however, remain socially backward with little education.

There is paucity of literature regarding their social structure. But in the institutional context, it is imperative to state that, by and large, they live in joint families, practice monogamy and observe patrilineal rules of lineage and patrilocal rules of residence. Such practices are relevant to them in the establishment of their status and identity in relation to other ethnic groups. They are also divided on the basis of religion. There are Hindu Gujjars too. The distinction between the Hindu and Muslim Gujjar is based on their way of life. The former claims Chamba as their homeland whereas the latter category is described as homeless (Singh, 1981: 18). Such a distinction also creates another type of hierarchy in which the native groups are ranked higher than the nomadic. One of the reasons behind it being that with permanent settlement the appropriation of resources have also become an important dimension of this community.

Bhot or Bhod, numerically placed fourth in population hierarchy of the scheduled tribes of Himachal Pradesh, is comprised by people from the upper reaches of Kinnaur and Lahaul and Spiti. It is believed that like Kinnauras they emigrated from Tibet. One of the rationale behind this belief is that the physical appearance of Bhots is like that of Tibetans. Some of the locals attempt at establishing blood relations between the two. These types of beliefs, although based on the historical process of immigration of people to the lands of Kinnaur, but conjectural understanding about different groups cannot be ruled out. It may, however, be noted that in the history of Kinnaur one does come across Bhot empire which existed during 630-50 A.D. It is further believed that the descendants of Bhots ruled this area effectively till 908 A.D. (cf. Mamgain, 1971: 51). In this way, the contemporary Bhots can be inferred as the descendants of Bhot empire.

Another significant aspect of Bhots is that they were, historically, influenced by Kinnauri culture and civilisation. The cultural exchange took place mainly through social, friendly and matrimonial alliances (cf. Mamgain, 1971: 52). Not much literature is available on the Bhot community. Like other ethnic groups, it seems that the social structure of Bhot community is also characterised by caste system. This is evident from the fact that the Thakurs among the Bhots ruled Bhot empire and the tradition of dominance of one particular caste in a particular region is not much different from even today where despite democratic setup certain traditional elite castes occupy the echelons of power. Religion is another factor on the basis of which Bhots are distinguished from each other. They are divided into Hindus and Buddhists. Like the Hindu society at large, the concept of purity-pollution seems to be prevalent among them. Mamgain (1975: 62) maintains that it is common among Bhots to consider all the body below the waist as polluted, and if the skirt or foot of a Bhot ever touches food or water, it is considered defiled. The beliefs in purity and pollution are so strong that food or any other item considered as defiled is thrown away.

The other scheduled tribes, namely, Pangwal, Swangla, Jad or Khampa or Lama and the Lahaula, represent numerically invisible minority in relation to the aforesaid scheduled tribes of Himachal Pradesh. Like the majority scheduled tribes, they are internally differentiated and stratified groups with a well-defined hierarchy of roles and status within the framework of their social structure. The restrictions on both the commensal and connubial relationships are strictly imposed by the social structure. The Khampas, traditionally nomads, started a settled life after Chinese aggression. They have been, by and large, carrying out petty business activities along with agriculture. Most of them are also engaged in low prestige occupations. The Pangwals, basically the inhabitants of Pangi in Chamba, due to severe climatic conditions, have remained underdeveloped in comparison to other scheduled tribes.

According to data on religious denominations (Census, 1991) most of the Bhots or Bhods spread all over Himachal Pradesh represent Buddhism as their main religion. The number of Hindus among them is a little above one-tenth of their total population. This, therefore, implies the pronounced impact of Buddhist religion and culture on them. This also establishes their historical links with Tibet where Buddhism has been the main religion. Gaddis on the other hand are predominantly Hindus. The representation of other religious faiths amongst them is almost nil. The Gujjars comprise Hindus and Muslims. The number of former is much higher than the latter. The Jads or Khampa or Lambas, like Bhots, also represent Buddhism as their major religion though it is difficult to ignore the regional variations. In Lahaul and Spiti and Chamba, majority of them return themselves as Buddhists.

Similarly, the majority of the people in Kinnaur are Hindus and so is the case with Kinnaura tribe. It is said that initially there was a Kinnaura tribe. With the advent time and development of division of labour among the Kinnauras the caste names started appearing. It is also said that social structure, however, was not without divisions prior to the development of castes. There used to be two major divisions, namely, Khasia and Chamang. The concept of Rajput and Koli was not known. It is later, particularly with the administrative impositions of the outside administrators that the Khasias were described as Rajputs and Chamangs as Kolis or the low castes or known as scheduled castes in the contemporary times. Similarly, another category called as Domangs (who followed blacksmithy) was added to the Kinnauras social structure. It is noted that these were not separate people but those from amongst the Khasias and Chamangs who went in for training in smithy (Negi, 1972). These castes, besides the socio-economic factors, determine the social structure of Kinnaura society. The third category, a religious one among Kinnaura is of Buddhists. Their percentage is around one-fourth of the total population of Kinnaur. Regional variations are also quite visible in them also. In Chamba, there are almost cent-per cent Hindus, whereas in Lahaul and Spiti region, they numerically represent their equal division into Hindus and Buddhists. But in the Kinnaur district they are roughly in the ratio of 70:30 as Hindus and Buddhists respectively. The Pangwals and Swanglas are also predominantly Hindus. Other religious faiths represent a small fraction of the total population.

A brief description of data indicates that principally three religions dominate among the scheduled tribes. But their domination is region specific, caused and conditioned by the historical process of their ecological settlement. Although Hinduism did have its influence on people coming from Tibet but they also brought Buddhism along with them. Buddhism which originated from India, in fact, flourished more in the other countries of south-east Asia.

To sum up, the spatial distribution of population indicates that Kinnaur, Lahaul and Spiti and Chamba districts are the three principal areas of tribal concentration. The Chamba district, however, has much less tribal population than Kinnaur and Lahaul and Spiti. These differences are caused by the rationale of 50 per cent or more tribal population for the declaration of scheduled tribes areas. Outside these areas, only Bilaspur and Kullu districts have somewhat visible tribal population. In other districts, the tribal have only fractional representation and they exist as invisible minorities. Another conspicuous feature about spatial distribution is the rural concentration. Out of the total tribal population, 98.41 per cent reside in rural areas. Only 1.59 per cent reside in the urban areas and that too outside the scheduled areas. It is also noted that the entire tribal belt in Himachal Pradesh remains rural so far. The process of urbanisation is very slow. The people in majority are dependent on primary sector (mainly agriculture) of economy. The commercial cropping, particularly cash crops like fruits, vegetables, etc., have become quite popular with the people in the recent times.

Patterns of Population Growth and Fertility Differentials in Himachal Pradesh

Today Himachal Pradesh ranks fourth among the states having lowest population growth. The decennial rate of growth of population in the state recorded in the census of 1991 was 19.39, higher than only Kerala (13.98), Tamil Nadu (14.94) and Goa (15.96). It is further worth mentioning that among the other hill states, Himachal Pradesh has the lowest population growth rates. One of the reasons accounting for this is the development which Himachal has achieved in the social sector, i.e., in education, health, etc. However, this existing rate, as is also true of all other states in India today, stands much higher than what it was in the beginning of the century. The decade-wise data since 1901 shown in Table 1.3 indicate considerable variation. It is found that in 1901-11, the growth of population in this hill state was

Table 1.3

Decennial Variation in Population since 1901

State/ District	*1901-11*	*1911-21*	*1921-31*	*1931-41*	*1941-51*	*1951-61*	*1961-71*	*1971-81*	*1981-91*
	Percentage Variation in Population								
Himachal	-1.22	+1.65	+5.23	+11.54	+5.42	+17.87	+23.04	+23.71	+19.39
Chamba	+6.68	+4.74	+3.48	+15.81	+0.08	+23.72	+16.34	+23.86	+25.68
Kangra	-1.95	+0.04	+5.41	+13.85	+1.33	+15.17	+21.85	+23.71	+16.05
Hamirpur	-1.95	+0.04	+5.41	+13.85	+1.33	+15.17	+20.26	+19.91	+13.08
Una	-1.95	+0.04	+5.41	+13.85	+1.33	+15.17	+15.29	+21.45	+18.03
Bilaspur	+2.46	+5.26	+3.06	+9.25	+14.29	+25.94	+22.66	+26.99	+17.80
Mandi	+3.20	+1.41	+11.07	+14.22	+2.29	+23.70	+34.07	+25.17	+19.17
Kullu	+4.36	-2.22	+7.70	+4.40	+6.19	+4.97	+25.79	+24.10	+26.39
Lahaul and Spiti	+4.75	-1.12	+6.99	+6.27	+5.10	+54.40	+16.41	+16.44	-3.99
Shimla	-2.80	+1.98	+4.45	+8.97	+10.19	+19.35	+22.96	+21.70	+20.35
Solan	-0.73	+11.52	-5.70	+8.31	+31.54	+14.50	+23.28	+27.71	+25.05
Sirmaur	+2.09	+1.39	+5.78	+5.02	+6.44	+18.93	+24.02	+25.30	+23.43
Kinnaur	+4.55	-0.98	+8.00	+9.17	+3.72	+18.87	+21.61	+19.49	+19.12

Source: Census of India, 1991, Himachal Pradesh.

in negative (-1.22). However, the population started increasing with a growth rate of +1.65 during the decade 1911-21. One of the reasons behind this population increase was the incoming of people from other states along with the British. Afterwards, it increased almost three times during the next decade, i.e., 1921-31. It doubled by 1931-41 and decreased once again almost to the level of 1921-31 in the next decade. From 1951-61, it increased at a rapid rate of 17.87, 23.04 in 1961-71 and 23.71 during 1971-81. The major reason for rapid increases, particularly in the decade 1951-61 was the reorganisation of the state and merger of erstwhile Punjab hill states with Himachal Pradesh. However, with the ongoing programmes in family planning, child and mother care and other activities, the population growth rate in the state declined to 19.39. Another important dimension of population growth in Himachal Pradesh is the inter-district variations in the size as well as the growth rates.

In the early years of the twentieth century, five districts of the state, namely, Kangra, Hamirpur, Una, Shimla and Solan had negative growth rates. In the following decade Kullu, Lahaul and Spiti, and Kinnaur had negative growth of population. Prior to which these districts were among those experiencing positive growth rates. However, from the decade 1921-31, except for Solan the population of all other districts was on the rise. The data, however, point out that the fluctuations in the rates of population growth could not be natural but were due to certain other factors affecting the population movement. It is obvious from the case of Solan during the three decades (1901-11 to 1921-31).

Further analysis of data indicates that from 1931-41 onward, the population of different districts of Himachal Pradesh experienced positive growth rates. During the this decade the maximum growth was taking place in Chamba, Kangra, Hamirpur, Una and Mandi districts. The next decade (1941-51), however, found the earlier trends changed. The districts having maximum growth found themselves with minimum rates of growth in their population. On the other hand, district like Solan experienced maximum increase in its population (31.54%). One of the reasons behind it being large number of people settling down in this town, especially with the shifting of government offices to this place. Interestingly, districts like Kangra, Hamirpur, Una, etc., showed much less growth in comparison to the previous decade. The reasons for these wide ranging variations in the rates of population growth, as has been said earlier, were not based on births. But these were due to the process of reorganisation of the erstwhile princely states. In some cases, it was due to mergers. In other cases, it was due to shifting of the central and Punjab government offices. In fact, it may also be noted that during the pre-partition period, all the districts listed in Table 1.3 and mentioned in the discussion were not even in existence. They came into being only after the process of reorganisation of the state which began during the British period and in the post-independence era when Himachal Pradesh attained complete statehood. During these times, some areas were merged with others, thus affecting the population size of that area.

It was only after 1951 that the state as well as its various districts, excepting Kullu and Lahaul and Spiti, experienced somewhat stable population growth. Although variations are quite obvious in the case of all the districts, but these are very wide in the case of Kullu and Lahaul and Spiti during the two decades, i.e., between 1951-61 and 1961-71. It has been found that the variations in the population of Kullu district and that of Lahaul and Spiti are caused by the migrations of people of the Lahaul and Spiti to Kullu during the winters and back to Lahaul and Spiti during the summers. The people of the latter maintain double residence due to harsh weather conditions in the Lahaul valley. During the decades 1971-81 and 1981-91, the population of all the districts of Himachal Pradesh, excepting Chamba and Kullu, declined. One of the reasons cited for the increase in the population of Chamba is the coming of Kashmiri immigrants. In the case of Kullu, this increase in the population growth is conditioned by the coming of the people from Lahaul and Spiti. Interestingly, the population growth in Lahaul and Spiti during 1981-91 was -3.99 in comparison to +16.44 during the decade 1971-81. These types of variations are caused more by spatial movement of population rather than by the natural rates of decline in population.

In Himachal Pradesh's scheduled tribes districts, Kinnaur is the one which has been having more stable growth or decline in population since 1951-61 onwards. This, may be called as the notable feature of Kinnaur, is indicated by the minimum fluctuation shown by data between 1961 to 1981-91. The rate has been +21.61, +19.49 and +20.48 respectively. Another dimension of population of Kinnaur before 1951 was that the population growth fluctuated much more than the post-independence phase. The reasons cited for such fluctuations in population of the district include wrongly returning as Kinnaura at the time of population enumeration, inclusion of those in the census who were living in the district due to one reason or the other, and inclusion of those in the district population who were not even living there (Negi, 1972). One of the plausible explanation also comes from the ongoing process of development projects. A considerable number of officials and specialised labour has also been coming to this region from time to time. How far has it been affecting the fluctuations cannot be said but it certainly made addition to the population of the district. The presence of outside population has been there in Kinnaur right from the pre-independence days.

Sex-ratio also constitutes an important dimension of any population. One of the implications sex-ratio has is for the institution of marriage. It is noted by some scholars that wherever the number of women is lesser than that of the males, polyandrous marriages, either open or in hidden manner, become more prevalent. Where the number of women exceeds men the possibility of polygyny cannot be ruled out. Polyandry prevailed in many parts of Kinnaur in the past. In the contemporary times, it has been, by and large, replaced by monogamous marriages. However, the formerly solemnised such marriages and the families based on such a system do exist in the present times. Some of the observations based on the fieldwork indicate polyandry prevailing in some families as a private affair. The reasons for its prevalence suggest that historically it was practised to prevent over-population and subdivisions and fragmentation of landholdings.

The patterns of sex-ratio in Kinnaur indicate that in 1901 it stood at 911 females per 1,000 males. It increased to 935 in 1921 and declined to 910 in 1931. In the subsequent years it increased to 940 in 1941 and 1070 in 1951. The later trends indicate gradual decline to 969, 893, 885 and 859 in the year 1961, 1971, 1981 and 1991 respectively. To what extent was sex-ratio responsible for polyandry cannot be stated. The data on sex-ratio in time-series context indicates prevalence of polyandry more when the sex-ratio was also high and more monogamous marriages when sex-ratio has been declining. It, therefore, suggests that more than the availability of women, it was family property considerations which might have been responsible for such a practice. Although it requires a detailed investigation into the relationship between sex-ratio and marriage practices, the indirect evidence suggests that prevalence and non-prevalence of polyandry has been influenced more by social and economic factors rather than by sex-ratio.

In the light of the foregoing analysis of patterns of population in Himachal Pradesh in general and tribal area with special reference to tribal areas of the state in particular, Kinnaur is chosen for the purpose of the study. The choice is made as the present study tends to concentrate on tribal demography. In order to examine the fertility behaviour in Kinnaur, it is also desirable to understand the existing theoretical formulations as well as literature on the relationship between social structure and fertility. This is also vital from the point of view of developing an appropriate methodology of the study. Another significant dimension which should form part of analysis is the women in Kinnaur and their work involvement. Following this the next chapter concentrates on the theoretical issues in demographic literature on social structure and fertility behaviour.

2 Social Structure and Reproductive Behaviour

The underlying assumption of this chapter is that social structure and fertility behaviour have a definite relationship which is mediated by social structural variables. Among these, the status of women is assumed to be a significant intervening factor. This chapter, therefore, attempts at understanding the concept of social structure, its constituent elements and the status of women and how these variables are related with fertility behaviour.

The concept of social structure in sociology in particular, though means differently to different people, yet in general implies a patterned set of social relationships expressed either through the role relationships and levels of interaction between various segments of population or in terms of relationships between various social classes formed on the basis of their economic position, the amount of power they have, the authority they exercise in relation to others and privileges they enjoy by virtue of their respective position in the social hierarchy of the society. It is, however, important to mention that the concept of social structure is not too general a phenomenon. It is quite complex as, besides being constituted by a large number of elements, it also has both the time (e.g., feudalism, capitalism, etc.), and space (e.g., Indian society, American society, etc.) dimension. Its explanation, therefore, needs to be in a specific social context.

In the Indian context, whether one may agree or not, social structure combines both the segmental divisions and class stratification. The former refers to castes and tribes graded and ranked on the basis of sacred attributes such as ritual purity and impurity, and the latter signifies the structured social hierarchy based on the secular dimensions, namely, social, economic and political. Some of the explanations, at times, take into consideration both sacred and secular dimensions for the purposes of ranking and social stratification. The reason for combining both the dimensions lies in the fact that Indian society is in transition and there prevails not one but multiple modes of social, economic and political organisation. The heterogeneity in the levels of development of different states and areas make it further difficult to delineate as to which mode is predominant at a given place and point of time. The caste and class dimensions of Indian social structure in certain situations transcend each other. In the same manner, one also finds multiple factors underlying the social structure of a tribal society located in a given socio-cultural, economic and political setting.

The cultural anthropologists, particularly Radcliffe-Brown explained the concept of social structure in terms of functions performed by its various parts. It is argued that social structure in itself is nothing but an agglomeration of various elements interacting in a systematic manner with each other and contributing to the well-being of the total structure. The reference to Radcliffe-Brown is neither to discuss the underlying postulates of functionalism or to glorify them but to make it implicit here that it is the systematic interaction between various parts of the whole which gives rise to a structure. It, therefore, implies that in understanding social structure detailed analysis of various constituent elements, especially of those which are highly relevant, is inevitable.

It also seems pertinent to mention that whether one looks at the concept of social structure from purely functional or structural, or structural-functional or/and Marxist point of view, the contents of analysis are always constituted by certain categories. In the case of functional and structural-functional conception, the categories exist as interrelated opposites. Since they are related with each other, these opposites are complementary to each other. However, in Marxism, the opposition is always a conscious creation of those who own and control means and forces of production. Such oppositions, which are based on antagonistic interests operate in a given historical juncture of society's material development and exist as parts of the superstructure. But the opposition, due to internal and external contradictions, is effectively mediated through certain intervening forces during the process of reproduction of material conditions of social life. It is our considered opinion that although the superstructural categories are determined by infrastructure yet these are significant in influencing the behaviour of human beings. Hence, there is a need for their conceptual understanding.

Among the constituent categories of social structure, social status and social role are the two most important dimensions. Since the society evolves a scheme of social stratification, there emerges a definite type of social structure in which different types of social stratum and roles come into being. These are not homogeneous categories but heterogeneous having oppositions within. This can be explained in terms of role conflicts which are often witnessed when an individual occupying more than one status confronts this problem. However, as distinct categories, role and social status in relation to each other act as complementary concepts and form part of the superstructure. In other words, these are determined by a multiplicity of factors. However, at the same time, both are critical in the determination of the life chances and styles of the individuals and the groups.

The aforementioned terms, i.e., social role and social status can be explained with the help of varying conceptions of the concept of social status. Coser and Rosenberg (1976: 276) argue that status is problematic when roles are vaguely defined. This indicates that in defining status one has to guard against various contradictions which it may present in terms of overlapping of terms and their multiple usage. One of the problems in the explanation of the term status is that of the context. In a formal setting characterised by achievement orientation, the explanation of social status is more explicit. But, in an informal setting where the position of the individual is determined on the basis of ascription, the status of the person remains vague, especially in the contemporary times when the other status determinants are also actively interacting. It is, therefore, felt that the status of the person in the inter-group context becomes ambiguous. Linton (1936) referring to the problems involved argues that the term status, like the term culture is being used with a double significance. Elaborating it further, he remarks that status, in the abstract, is a position in a particular pattern. But the meaning becomes more clear only when the term is qualified. Otherwise, the status of any individual means the sum total of all the status he occupies in the social structure of the society (Linton, 1936, cited in Coser and Rosenberg, 1976: 277). Thus, there is a need to make use of the term in a specific manner and in relation to the given social and cultural setting.

In contrast to the above explanations, Marx, often described as the one who for the first time made use of the term 'social class' in explaining the social structure of the society, refers to the status of individuals and groups based on particular type of mode of production. Marx's viewpoint suggests that the class is significant in the determination of the position or the role of an individual or groups in the given social structure of the society. He refers to two common grounds for this. First, the class position of the individual in the given mode of production is specific and that specificity defines his role. Second, the position which the group occupies in the power structure of the state is important to determine his position in relation to the resources of the society. In view of which Marx seems to lay emphasis on the economic situation of the individual, power they hold—mainly political power, along with their social position which determine their social status in the society (Tumin, 1987: 9-12). Marxist explanation, despite guided by his historical-materialism method is viewed by critics as one-sided.

Max Weber who attempted to repudiate Marx, looks at social status in terms of prestige differences prevailing in a society. The prestige of an individual is not necessarily based on his economic attributes or position. The economic aspect may constitute just one aspect of the complete reality. However, the critical appraisal of what Weber argues may indicate that prestige enjoyed by an individual in the society is not independent of his social class, the power and authority enjoyed by him in relation to others. In fact, in the context of the influence which all the three may have on each other, Weber has himself argued, "parties may represent interests determined through class situation or status situation... but they need to be neither purely 'class', not purely 'status', 'parties'...". It, therefore, implies that status is not based on one attribute of the life of the individual but may involve other aspects too (Tumin, 1987: 14).

It becomes quite pertinent to mention here that Weber's ideas carried considerable influence in the analysis of social status of individuals. This approach with particular reference to the American society was used by Warner and others who conducted a study in Yankee City. They followed Weber's thesis of honour and prestige as important components in the determination of social status. The variables considered vital in social status included income, occupation, style of living, and so on. In addition to the said, the status differentiation was also found to be caused by the educational attainments of the people. All these variables as individual or group acquisitions enable an individual or a group to occupy a particular social status in relation to others in the society. In this way, there also emerges a social structure containing different social classes.

One of the methodological issues in the context of social structure and fertility behaviour is---whose social status is crucial? Is it the husband or the wife or the family as unit whose status matters? It is well known that understanding of population dynamics falls within the broad purview of demography, which is the scientific study of populations, their size, composition, distribution, and change. The change in population and its various dimensions depends on fertility, mortality and migrations. Fertility, a biological phenomenon, is basic to the population of any given society. It implies the number of children a woman bears during her life-time. This is different from fecundity which means the number of children a woman is capable of bearing during her life-time. It is noticeable from the very meaning of the term that women is central to fertility. It is, therefore, her status which, hypothetically, should matter most.

The status of a woman herself, especially in a patriarchal society, is dependent on the man, family and the social structure. In the modern human society, as explained above, social status of an individual depends on a multiplicity of factors. Woman, as a distinct social category, is not merely a biological or sexual being but also a gender category. In terms of her sexuality, a woman represents the anatomical differences between a male and a female. As a gender category, it is concerned with the psychological, social and cultural differences in the socialisation and personality makeup between a male and a female. This distinction between sex and gender arises due to the differential psychological, social and cultural conditioning of men and women in the society, and not on the basis of biological or bodily differences. The differences are created in the society by the people themselves and are the product of social structural factors (Giddens, 1995: 161-62). It, therefore, implies that the status of women, besides their economic and prestige attributes, also depends upon the social and cultural milieu in which they are placed. This difference is of considerable value in the study of demographic behaviour. The basic reason being that social and cultural factors influence the desire for a particular sex of the progeny. It, therefore, implies that in defining the status of women as high and low the cultural values associated with the female in a given social structure are of considerable importance.

The Ford Foundation (1991), with particular reference to women and fertility, described status of women in terms of a women centered approach. The variables of measuring status of women, according to this approach are education, nutritional status, dignity in the society, i.e., the social recognition of women and their work, access to food and medical care, length of pregnancy intervals, number of children born including stillbirths, premature abortions, number of survivals, maternal mortality, control over sexuality---early or late exposure, decision-making about the number of children, cultural values such as age at marriage, social norms governing life of women, income, occupational status, right to spacing and number of children, etc. This list of status variables affecting reproductive health and fertility behaviour is apparently quite exhaustive and covers all aspects of social status of an individual in general and status of women with particular reference to fertility behaviour.

The question of women's social status is not simple to understand as there are numerous variations conditioned by the varying existential conditions of women in human society in general and in specific type of social habitats, namely, tribal communities, slum-dwellers, etc. Theoretically, there are also two juxtaposed conditions of women's life. First, there is a common place observation that women are excluded from social, economic and political spheres of the society. Consequently, they are denied all the privileges which they may have been enjoying if the said privileges were extended to them and a result of which they would have had a social status equal to that of men. At times, it is also felt that what to talk of equality, they are even considered inferior and subordinate to men in all walks of life. Such a view is often legitimised by describing them as physically and otherwise weaker than men. The stereotypes prevalent about them in the society render women as incapable of doing the things which the men can do (see Rosaldo and Lamphere, 1974).

The second viewpoint, drawing evidence from the history of human society seems to suggest that women have been dominant at some stage of evolution of the society. Consequently, they did enjoy certain privileges and held political power. The historically inconsistent status situation of women, however, gives rise to an issue that if they had higher social status then why were they reduced to a status of subordination in relation to men. Related with this is another issue that why in some societies at certain point of time they were accorded a high social status and in some other societies at the same time they had a lower social status.

There are numerous theoretical explanations which take into consideration the socio-economic and socio-cultural dimensions of human society and the placement of women within it. One such viewpoint states that wherever women enjoy control over the outcome of their labour and participate in collective decision-making they enjoy a high social status. This means that through work participation and collective decision-making the women enjoy certain amount of authority over the others. It is with the use of this authority, whatever its nature and quantum may be, the women are able to influence others and their decisions (see Sanday, 1973; Reiter, 1975). At the same time, it is also believed that having certain amount of authority and participation in the work does not get a woman high social status. The reason being that much depends on how a society views women's participation in work. It is a sociologically recognised fact, as Weber would put, that the social status to a considerable extent also depends on the social and cultural attributes of the person or the group concerned. Whether women command high status by participating in the work or they do not depend on the values attached with work in a particular social setting.

From the anthropological point of view the subordinate position of women is the result of the process of social evolution of human society. Levi-Strauss argues that when a society comes into being the interaction between different groups starts taking place. In this process, the women, for the material exchange value attached with them, act as the source of facilitation of social interaction between the groups. This exchange during the said times was not merely in terms of woman as a human body meant for sexual pleasure and carrying on the reproductive activities. Rather, it also acted as a medium of cultural exchange as it was accompanied by exchange of cultural patterns and practices, ancestral rights and social structural aspects of different groups between whom the exchange took place. In this way, the values attached with women put them in a position comparable with other physical objects. The patriarchy and patriarchal system of authority makes the process of equating women with other material objects easier and faster. The perpetuation of patriarchy in a constant manner denied women of their right over the household property and other material valuables. This further resulted in the undermining of women's position in relation to men and their deliberate exclusion from the decision-making processes of the family (see Maine, 1961).

Could matriarchy or matriarchal system as an alternative provide higher social status to women? It is noted that the time when the women were supposed to have been dominant was, perhaps, when matriarchy existed in human society. The historical evidence, however, suggests that matriarchy had a temporary and brief existence in some parts of the world and that too for a very short-period. It is also maintained that even during the period matriarchy prevailed the males must have had held higher position than women, particularly in the economic and political affairs of the society. It is interesting to refer to the case of native women in Canada who at one point of time held complete control over fur trade. They dealt with the foreign customers, negotiated costs and determined prices and so on. But male domination over them remained as they did not have the right over the property. In other words, even during the matriarchy the women enjoyed more autonomy not for themselves but for the running of the family economy. In this way, they had more autonomy than the women who were fully dependent on men. Even in the case of some of the tribes of the north-eastern Indian states where matriarchy prevails, the men dominate, particularly in economic production and political participation and decision-making processes. A woman may be dominant in the house, in the *mohalla* (neighbourhood) or the village but her power is limited, especially when she comes to exercise of the power in relation to man.

Marxist thesis regarding the low social status of women is centred around the basic premises of property relations. The main issue discussed in this context is as to who owns and controls family property. It is a well-known fact that Marx did not deal with the gender question in specific. However, one of his remarks in *Eighteenth Brumaire of Louis Bonaparte* does reflect about his concern for the highly vulnerable position of women and their subsequent exploitation. He argued that nations and women are not spared in their unguarded hours, particularly when a more adventurous warrior is around. The implication of this argument is that the possibility of women's exploitation always exists. The women, whether it was case of a feudal or a capitalist society, they were always exploited by men and the society at large.

In Marxism, the subjugation of women is traced from the process of historical and materialistic development of society. Marx draws our attention towards the precarious and vulnerable condition of women, particularly in the context of women's participation in the capitalist production and acting as a unit of capitalist productive system. While developing a viewpoint on women's status, Engels, in his book, *The Origin of Family, Private Property and the State*, argues that there exists a relationship between property management, patriarchal system and the government. It is argued that the capitalist production process reduces a woman from a free-equal productive member of the society to a subordinate and dependent wife. It is, however, difficult to argue whether men and women prior to capitalist production were equal or not. Engels' thesis, however, is that the human society at all times has been dependent on men and women in an equal manner for production and procreation. This also logically suggests a definite relationship between the production and procreation.

Having discussed at length the concept of social structure, social status and status of women, it is assumed that in studying fertility behaviour, especially in the Indian context and with reference to women, both the sacred and the secular dimensions of a social structure are significant. This is particularly so when one is confronted with questions: What is the role of social and cultural values in the child-bearing practices of a group? Does there prevail an economic rationality in making a decision regarding bearing a child or an additional child? Maras refers to micro-analytical theories and macro-analytical theories. The former deals with issues such as individual survival or life span, variations in individual survival and life span, and the causes and the correlates of both. The other concern is to understand the fertility of individuals and couples, variations in number and spacing of births, and causes and correlation of such variations. The macro-analytical theories on the other hand explore societal patterns of fertility and mortality, and the structural and institutional features of societies which bear upon survival, mortality and fertility. The scope of the micro-analytical theories remains limited as these are not in a position to spell out what exactly determines the reproduction of social and cultural life and then how these further influence variations. In other words, one of the question related with causes of fertility is: Where are the causes located---in the individual or the social structure in which he is placed with specific lifestyles and life chances?

The existing inadequacy of micro-analytical theories calls

for an alternative perspective. The macro-analytical theories seem to fill the void. One of the reasons being that these theories attempt at locating the reasons of fertility and mortality in the social structure and the institutions. The latter is crucial in the analysis of social organisation of life of a community and the social practices. The study of social institutions, according to Malinowski (1932), is important as these are the most stable element of social structure, express culture and through which reflect on the structure. His rationale behind selecting social institutions as crucial was guided by his understanding that these were the permanent features of a society and reflect adequately on the cultural practices of the people. In the context of what is more suited to the study of fertility behaviour, Maras in summing up the role of macro and micro-analytical theories argues that the role of social conditions in the very fact are important in decision-making about marriage, family formation and number of births.

The foregoing discussion on the concepts of social structure, social status, and the status of women reveals certain constraints of social structure, culture and economy on the life of women. These not only affect their social status but also influence women's biological functions, particularly those related with reproduction. In South Asia, women status and the state of their physical existence have a definite bearing on fertility. In rural areas, the social structure denies access to and control of productive resources to women. The significant differences between men and women in relation to productive resources affect the recognition of women's work even by planners and policy-makers. It is observed that by considering only the behaviour of males or assuming that it somehow accounts for female behaviour also, planners have only half the information base needed for determining population policy (see, Zeidenstein, 1991). The society just does not end up with the property inequalities but creates a structure of unequal values attached to sons and daughters throughout in the rural South Asia. In India, in some of the regions, minimum one son is a must as some of the functions related with lifecycle rites and rituals are to be performed by the son only.

The structural constraints resulting in general denial of property rights to women and the utilisation of their income for the advancement of educational interests of the sons respectively is based on the basic motive of the parents that their sons would act as a security during their old age (Cairns and Greenhalgh, cited in PCAR 1991). How do this affect fertility is found in the reproductive behaviour of families in rural setting. To beget sons, the women are made to produce more children. The compulsion, as the studies seem to suggest, arises basically due to two reasons. First, the social and cultural values attached with sons and consequential discrimination against the women. Second, no control of women over their bodies and productivity makes them vulnerable to men's decision about the number of children.

It may be mentioned that the population council way back in 1989 took note of the general tendency of the human society "not to recognise the significance of women's work in the economy of the family". It, thus, laid emphasis on the recognition of the economic contribution made, both by men and women, to the families resources. The fact otherwise remains that the women do much more than the men. Bruce (1979) said, "The women who head families and the employed mothers devote many hours and much energy to the earning of income while not relieved of the traditional burden of looking after other chores, particularly the children." This is basically due to the limited access that the women have to economic resources in the family. The women's productive and reproductive roles to

Llyod are, in fact, related with three factors, viz., women's ability to gain access to a secured income, solid support from father for their children, and control over their fertility (Llyod cited in PCAR 1991).

The Ford Foundation (1991) emphasised that women status is important in the determination of fertility. The reason being that women's status can act as a key factor in their ability and desire to control fertility. Sivard (1985, quoted in FF 1991: 9) argues: "Women must be able to achieve social status and dignity, to manage their own health and sexuality, and to exercise their basic rights in society and in partnership with men." The Ford Foundation document also points out that many women are prevented from achieving this status by legal, social, and cultural norms or the structure of rules and regulations guiding various practices in a society. Therefore, it implies that an understanding of relationship between women status and fertility must also take into consideration the social structure influencing the both.

In addition to the above, Spengler (1966: 109-30) refers to biological, and the social and economic conditions. The former related with involuntary biological factors and the latter involves voluntary decision-making process regarding child-bearing practices. The importance of the second aspect lies in the fact that fertility, sex preferences, expenditure involved in the child bearing and rearing are carefully considered. Much depends upon the income of the couple. It is quite discernible that in the case of modernised and industrially advanced society where the general literacy level is high, child bearing, by and large, is a rational social action. It may also be added that woman's general employment status and how much she can afford to forego in terms of income remains very significant factor.

Srinivasan (1988) made projections about the impact of alternative trends in population growth on key sectors of economy and society. He argued that there exists a direct relationship between the minimum required standards of economy and the fertility levels. The higher rate of population growth aggravates inequalities in income and consumption patterns of basic goods and services. Since the status of an individual is determined on the basis of level of income and patterns of consumption of material things, it is likely that these factors would also affect the fertility behaviour.

Zacharia and Nag (1983) in the context of Kerala refer to the highly significant relationship between income and fertility. While lowest fertility was found to be in the middle income groups, the upper income groups showed intermediate levels and the lowest income group indicated highest level of fertility. The basic reason for the lowest fertility in the middle income group was that the most people exposed to the strains of urbanisation and modernisation, as well as most preoccupied by the desire to educate their children and the aspirations for a better life tended to have fewer children. Similarly, changes in income distribution either because of land reforms or otherwise were also found to be related with declining fertility in India (Ratcliffe 1978; Mencher 1980; Zachariah 1983).

At the same time, there has also been some debate on the issue above referred to. Ratcliffe indicates that implementation of land reforms raised wage level of women in Kerala and thereby reduced fertility among the poor. Contrary to this view has been the assertion made by Mencher and Zachariah that the implementation of land reform legislation in Kerala had led to the decline in the fertility through privation and aggravation of housing problems. Such shortages created widespread acceptance of family planning in order to reduce desired family size and caused postponement of marriage by the older children because they could not find housing.

Women education, another variable significant in determining social status, is also found to be positively associated with reduction in fertility According to Jain (1985), the impact of education has not only been confined to urban India but also to the rural areas. Rural India's total fertility rates decreased with the increase in female education. Higher school enrollment ratios, particularly those of females have been associated with various elements contributing to decline in fertility rates. These elements include higher female age at marriage, the improved status of women and a higher rate of family planning practices.

Sharma (1987), in a longitudinal study, highlights the social and institutional controls affecting the fertility. These include non-marriage of women, changing age at marriage or the late marriages, taboos on widow remarriages and other religious and ritualistic practices. Along with the aforesaid, Sharma also suggests certain other variables which are important in determining fertility. These are improvement in birth control technology and expansion of the health care system. Both the factors are conducive to better health status of women which substantially affect their general social status.

Jain and Visaria (1988) edited a volume on infant mortality, mortality differentials and determinants. Since higher levels of mortality have been accounting for higher fertility in India, various research articles contributed by different scholars in the volume lay emphasis on all those factors which deal with women health and care. The study does not indicate any direct reference to fertility but has an indirect bearing on fertility which is closely associated with mortality.

Mahadevan and Sumangala (1987) refer to the effect of social development and cultural change on fertility behaviour. It is pointed out that in Kerala fertility rates are lower than the other states all over India. This could be possible due to improvement in quality of life of the people in terms of health, hygiene, literacy, and status of women. Patel (1990) studied the impact of modernisation on changes in levels of fertility. It is quite interesting to note that women as mothers-in-law have an important role to play in acceptance and non-acceptance of family planning devices. The uneducated and low caste mothers-in-law disapprove daughters-in-law undergoing sterilisation operation. Although the author does not explain why this is so, but the obvious reason seems to be that by undergoing sterilisation the woman would become incapable of bearing children. It is here that one can think of age difference between the mothers-in-law and the daughter-in-law as the intervening factor. However, the study indicates the change towards smaller family taking place in the attitude of educated and those who are exposed to urban way of life. The better educated and salaried couples adopt birth control techniques earlier than the others. It is, therefore, discernible that education and income of couples have considerable effect on fertility. But, the role of other structural factors, namely, socio-cultural, is of no less significance which at times also build up pressure for accepting the locally prevalent values about the number of children which the couple or the family must bear.

Hoem (1990) discussed the impact of social policy on fertility change in Sweden. The study basically tries to reflect a change in the time pattern of cohort fertility. The social policy in Sweden tends to provide financial incentive to those who practice close spacing of births. It may be noted that such a policy is adopted to expand the population base. The people in general in Sweden tend to have fewer children and that too with longer time gaps. By adopting such policies the country wants to increase its population. Since the employment rate for women is also high, the financial incentives, therefore, tend to reduce the financial loss which a woman may suffer because of going on a maternity leave due to childbirth. It is, therefore, women's employment which seems to have a definite bearing on the child-bearing practices among the Swedes. The reason being that if a woman takes leave from her job she has to sacrifice experience at job and forego skill development. That is the reason why women in employment in general have fewer children.

Aiyappan and Mahadevan (1990) examined the mortality and fertility of Kurichiyas, a tribal community of Waynad in Kerala. The study points out that this group has maintained its traditional structure and practices which also include respect for their women, absence of dowry and their matrilineal system. The other distinguishing feature of the Kurichiyas is that they maintain an egalitarian family management system and high status of women due to matrilineal inheritance of property rules. The evidence of decline in fertility is found among them. It is, however, noted that besides the status which the community accords to women there are certain restrictions on them which prevent them from having pre or extramarital relationships.

Sinding (1991) analysed fertility decline in Kenya and reported some of the factors which account for such trends. These are: (i) rapid social change with particular reference to increase in the educational level of women; (ii) greater governmental legitimisation of family planning; (iii) government officials', especially the bureaucrats' role in the distribution of contraceptives; and (iv) global acceptance of family planning programmes. Besides the aforementioned factors, economic crises sometimes also play a significant role by deferring marriages and increasing birth spacing. It is further argued that the factors underlying structural adjustment measures make not only the government but also individuals more aware of cost considerations in making reproductive and other behavioral choices. In this process, education and the rising economy are described as quite significant contributors in decline of fertility.

Govindasamy's (1992) analysis of ethnicity and fertility differentials in Malaysia indicate that the new economic policy which was not aimed at fertility but at the reduction of economic inequality in Malaysia, had an impact on the fertility behaviour of different ethnic groups. This study, therefore, refers to the fact that improvement in the socio-economic conditions can affect the fertility differentials in a significant manner.

Caldwell et al. (1992) argue that sexual system prevalent in a country also affects the fertility. In a country where women have liberty to go for premarital sexual relationship, the chances of pregnancy are always very high. On the contrary, in countries like India, China, Bangladesh, South Korea, Taiwan where strong proscriptions for female premarital sexual activity prevail it is likely to prevent teenage pregnancy and child births. The study, therefore, suggests that women status which is also measured in terms of their freedom and autonomy in a given socio-cultural setting give rise to the problem of high rate of child births. In other words, structurally determined norms, such as the degree of promiscuity, freedom with regard to premarital sexual relations, etc., result in corresponding levels of fertility behaviour.

An edited volume entitled *Family Planning Programme and Fertility* by Phillips and Ross (1992) and reviewed by Burch reveals that one should not discount the qualitative insights, many of which are provided by the volume at hand. A good programme may increase demand for fertility regulation, change preference for children, reduce fatalistic attitudes, and least, may help change in the position and self-image of women. The latter perhaps has its implications for enabling women to have control over their fertility.

Basu (1992) studied the relationship between culture, status of women and fertility behaviour of slum-dwellers of Delhi. The people living there had hailed from Uttar Pradesh and Tamil Nadu. The differences in their demographic behaviour were found to be more associated with their respective cultures than to their socio-economic conditions. Women status, which constituted core of the study, is defined in terms of the extent of women's exposure to the outside world, their interaction with the non-familial world and the degree of autonomy commanded by them in the decision-making process of the family. These factors are found to be associated with age at marriage, family size norms prevalent among them, etc. At the same time, the study also indicates that the role of culture seems to be more vital in determining the demographic behaviour than the status of women.

The International Conference on Population and Development held in 1994 devoted a full chapter to the theme---Gender Equality, Equity and Empowerment of Women. It emphasised that the empowerment of women and autonomy of women in the social, economic, political and health status is a highly important end in itself. Education is one of the means to empower women with knowledge, skills and self-confidence necessary to participate fully in the development process. The improvement in the status of women also enhances their decision making capacity at all levels in all spheres of life, especially in the area of sexuality and reproduction.

Malhotra, Vanneman and Kishor (1995) looked into the relationship between fertility, dimensions of patriarchy and development in India. They argue that fertility behaviour is often strongly related to gender inequality. Furthermore, these inequalities are embodied in the structure of the kinship and the culture in such a way that it becomes extremely difficult to undo the cultural pressures in bearing the children. The research conclude that social development *per say* may alter the patriarchal constructions despite structural resistance, and this alteration is worth the initiative required, both for raising women's position and for lowering fertility. In this way, the study suggests that women status has an inverse relationship with fertility. At the same time, it also points out that a number of socio-cultural factors too play a vital role in determining fertility. In other words, along with women status, the other structurally associated factors also affect fertility.

The foregoing review of studies indicate that social structure of a society and the socio-economic and cultural elements constituting social structure have a definite relationship with fertility behaviour. It is invariably noticed that most of the structural factors, especially income, education, occupation, age at marriage, social values attached with child birth and the sex of the child influence fertility considerably. Keeping in view various studies mentioned above the following hypotheses emerge for further analysis.

In general, it is hypothesised that social structure influences the child-bearing practices. The nature of influence, i.e., high or low fertility, depends more upon the type of social structure. It is assumed that a liberal social structure enabling women to have control over their bodies and make decisions about the number of children will lead to low fertility. On the other hand, a social structure which permits more of physical promiscuity and premarital relationships will lead to higher fertility. The levels and fertility differentials are also mediated by socio-economic variables which also constitute social structure.

The relationship between fertility behaviour and its determinants, however, is not simple but a very complex phenomenon. There is not one but multiple factors which influence and account for fertility in varying ways under varying conditions. Each factor seems to operate alone or in combination with others under certain conditions, thus, making understanding of the relationship very difficult. However, on the basis of trends indicated by the review of studies, it is further hypothesised that

---- women status is determined by the specific social and cultural conditions underlying the structure;

---- women's work participation inside and outside the family is generally high with low recognition in a society based on the values of patriarchy;

---- women's participation in the decision-making process is also generally low in a social structure conditioned by patriarchal values. However, differentials in the participation in decision-making are caused by the relative social and economic status of women;

---- the child-bearing practices are greatly influenced by the structure of social values conditioning marriage related practices; and

---- the fertility behaviour differentials are caused by socio-economic and value variations. In general, the relationship between these factors is found to be inverse in nature.

The foregoing discussion spelt out the hypotheses of this study. To what extent do these hypotheses hold true can be tested through an empirical exercise. It is possible by way of systematic observation of social life of the group or the community. This enables the researcher to find and understand differential patterns among what is observed (Babbie, 1992:2). Further elaboration of social research becomes possible with reference to structuring of the research problem. The latter involves exploration, description and explanation. What is being explored depends upon the relevance of the subject under study for the social order of the society, human groups and the individuals. The description refers to the elaboration of the situation or the phenomenon in a scientific manner with accuracy and precision. The explanation part pertains to the question of why a particular observed phenomenon prevails in a society as it has been observed. In this context, Babbie (1992:17) argues that there are two worlds of reality. First one is known and called as 'experiential reality' and second is the 'agreed reality' about which one learns on the basis of empirical analysis of the situation concerned.

The other important dimensions of any sociological research problem are its two aspects, namely, the conceptual and the procedural. According to Sharma (1997: 26-27), the conceptual aspect of the research problem deals with defining of the key concepts used in the study and their operationalisation in the field setting. Broadly speaking, this implies making clear the contextual connotation of the concepts used in the empirical setting. The second aspect refers to the techniques used in the systematic collection of data, analysis, application of statistical tools for the testing of associations or correlation, if any. The conceptual part has already been dealt at length in the earlier part of this chapter, this section, therefore, deals with the procedural aspects of the study.

Research design, basically, refers to the planning of scientific inquiry. In other words, it elicits the strategy to find or explore a phenomenon. It is argued that what is significant in this process is to specify what is being investigated and what is the best way of going about the research (cf. Babbie, 1991: 89). Since the present study, as the title itself suggests, primarily concerns with the social structure, status of women and fertility behaviour, it is imperative to follow both exploratory and descriptive research design. An exploratory research design is followed when the phenomenon under investigation has not been researched earlier, especially in the specific social, cultural and economic conditions of life or setting. This is, therefore, quite appropriate to follow this in the context of the Kinnaura women. Along with exploration, it is important to describe the researched and observed patterns. At this point, it is also worthwhile to mention that since there have been studies on fertility behaviour in general in areas other than Kinnaur, some tentative assumptions or hypotheses have been framed on the basis of secondary sources and the same will be put to an empirical test in the field setting.

Along with the above the analysis of social structure, status of women and fertility determinants are examined in the given cultural setting of Kinnaur district in Himachal Pradesh which as has been said earlier is the geographical area chosen for the study. The reason for placing the analysis in the cultural context implies that besides the socio-economic variables, the cultural factors also have determining effect. It is in view of this that it becomes important to look at the cultural aspects of women's status with particular reference to the socio-cultural practices of the study area. A brief discussion on this aspect has already been carried out in the first chapter, more discussion however will be done in the context of the needs of each of the chapters of the study.

Universe and the Sample of the Study

This study was conducted in Sungra, Nichar sub-division of

Kinnaur district. This area was chosen on random basis. After having made selection of one of the development blocks on random basis, one of the major villages of the area was chosen on the basis of three important dimensions. First, the village with maximum population was considered as an ideal choice as it provided structurally differentiated population with somewhat homogenous cultural setting. Second criterion was the level of development of the village. The underlying assumption here being that a village with higher level of development provides possible variations in the socio-economic status of women. Initially, three biggest villages were selected on the basis of their levels of development, two lesser developed villages were excluded. The village Sungra with highest scores on amenities was selected. The village, according to the latest listing of the voters list has approximately 1,300 households. A total number of 784 married women between the age of 18 and 49 years constituted the universe of the study. A total of 50 per cent, i.e., 392 of all the women falling in the said age group were selected as the sample of the study on random number basis.

The other part of the research methodology refers to the technical tools used in the collection of data. The present study is based on primary sources and data were collected through fieldwork. The basic technique used for the purpose of the data collection is interview schedule, which was constructed by keeping in view the conceptual components of the study which have been highlighted in the previous section. The interview schedule consisted of status variables which included age, caste, education, occupation, income, living conditions, facilities and household assets. In order to examine the life chances accessible to the study population, questions pertaining to certain infrastructure facilities such as health, education, transport, etc., were included in the next sections. The other parts of the interview schedule included questions on decision-making process in the family, marriage and child-bearing practices of the respondents with regard to their fertility behaviour. The last section of the interview schedule included questions on knowledge, acceptance and practices of family planning followed and observed in the study area. In this way, the main tool used for data collection in the study was interview schedule consisting of various parts. It is further mentioned that in order to make comparative analysis, the data were also collected by using the secondary sources, namely, reports and other relevant information from the office of the health department.

Before administering the schedule in the field setting the researcher carried out pre-testing of the interview schedule. On the basis of which the schedule was modified to suit the requirements of the study. In other words, the interview schedule was operationalised in the field setting. This minimised the chances of data errors and other type of deviations which very often occur in a field study. A total of 10 per cent of the sample was taken for the purposes of pre-testing.

In this study, the data were computed with the help of Statistical Package for Social Sciences (SPSS) on computer. The general frequency tables were prepared and the averages wherever necessary were calculated. The averages are calculated as these are considered to be point of balance (Simbson and Kalfka 1965: 163).

Since the study emphasises on the understanding of relationship between social structure and status of women, the social structural and status variables are associated with fertility behaviour. In this context, the percentages have been calculated in order to compare different categories. In this context, the chi-square test was applied to observe the difference of association between expected and the observed frequencies. It is obtained by taking the square of the difference between the observed and expected frequency in each cell. We divide this figure by expected number of the cases in order to standardise it. This is basically done when there are two comparative groups taken for the purposes of analysis. In this study the comparative data were prepared on the basis of various categories which emerged in the process of frequency distribution. In this way, the chi-square besides being used to see association was also used to see the strength of association which the variables may have with each other.

3 Structure, Culture and Women

The theoretical discussion on the relationship between social structure, women and fertility indicated definite linkages, not only between the trio but also with other conditions in which the human beings live. Methodologically, it is, therefore, assumed that in understanding fertility differentials the analysis of social, cultural and economic dimensions of a society and the group under study are not only desirable but constitute an essential condition. Since women are central in the process of reproduction and they live under specific social and cultural conditions underlying the social structure, their social status and behaviour is conditioned by the value structure of a society. In other words, the way women think, orient their life and act is not their own but imposed by the society or the social structure of which they are a part. Logically, it follows that women's work participation inside and outside the family is influenced by the conditions of their family. But the recognition of their work in a society characterised by the values of patriarchy, by and large, remain low. Since no value is attached to the work performed by women for their families, their participation in the decision-making process is also low and therefore, ineffective. However, differentials in the participation in decision-making are caused by the relative social and economic status of women.

In continuation of the aforementioned tentative hypotheses, this chapter analyses the socio-cultural dimensions of Kinnaura community with particular reference to status of women, their emerging social and economic profile, work participation and involvement in the decision-making process of the family.

Socio-cultural and Economic Conditions of Women

A brief discussion on the social structure of Kinnaur revealed that the people of this part have their own distinct social structure which combines the elements of a tribe as well as that of Hindu caste system. Their way of life is characterised by different types of marital practices, sexual behaviour, status of women, patterns of reproduction, sex preferences and local customs and traditions governing family size. Besides being a tribe, Kinnauras like any other segment of Hindu population, also practice caste system. The identification of people by nomenclatures, such as Khashias (non-scheduled castes, namely, Brahmin, Kshatriya, Rajput and Vaishya) and Beru (scheduled castes, namely, Chamar, Chuhra, etc.) is enough to indicate caste distinction and caste based stratification in a tribe.

It is a well-known fact that the status of an individual in the Indian rural setting in general is largely determined on the basis of caste. But caste as a factor of stratification in the case of a tribe may look strange but this does exist in Kinnaur. The descriptions available on this aspect in history and official documents, e.g., district gazetteer is substantiated by the empirical evidence collected during the course of fieldwork. All the respondents mentioned their caste. Of the total 67.6 per cent returned themselves as high caste (mainly Rajputs) and 32.4 per cent are scheduled castes. There are other castes too. The Brahmins also live in Kinnaur. It is due to a chance factor that no Brahman family came within the purview of the sample. In the status hierarchy, the Rajputs occupy high status and the scheduled castes have low social status.

The caste system prevailing in this area has been very strict. Like other regions of India, the caste also determined women's status and the nature of their work participation. It is generally found that if a woman married a man of high caste, her caste was also elevated. But in the Transgiri and Cisgiri areas a man who married a women of low caste was also downgraded and was destined to the lower caste. Since caste was also associated with a particular occupation, the caste status, therefore, affected work participation considerably. The extent and magnitude of impact of caste on participation in work is not highlighted in the available literature.

Along with caste, the institution of religion exists as an integral part of a tribe. Its presence among the tribes is conditioned by the coherence of beliefs and practices concerning the supernatural beings. The other reason being that religion had its origin in the minds of the primitive people who looked for alternatives to their most pressing problems. This is what Durkheim believed was collective representation of sentiments and beliefs. Even Marx termed religion as a superstructural phenomenon which is deeply rooted in the consciousness of human beings and acts as a sign of the oppressed. In other words, religion seems to have its origin in the conditions of distress faced by the human beings. It continues to be the part of a society due to the fact that it also provides a set of beliefs which to a considerable extent guide people's behaviour and most people respond to the beliefs even if these are irrational. In the context of fertility and sex preference, one of the beliefs among Hindus is that the birth of a son is a must for attaining salvation.

Likewise, religion and religious beliefs are a part of the life of the Kinnauras. They are divided into two main religions, namely, the Hinduism and Buddhism. Their life, right from birth till death, is conditioned by a number of customs, traditions and elaborate ritual system. The rituals are associated with events like child-birth, marriage and death. The role of Brahmin priest and the Buddhist *Lama* is of great significance in almost all aspects of social life of the people. It is also a fact that Kinnaur being located on the Tibetan border has considerable influence of Buddhism. The census of 1991 enumeration of religious denominations in the Kinnaur district of Himachal Pradesh reveals that besides 40 per cent of Hindus of the total population, Buddhists number 28.4 per cent. Although in the study sample the number of Buddhists is only 1.8 per cent, but its significance in the social and cultural life of Kinnaur is crucial. The small number of Buddhists in the sample is conditioned by the fact that majority of them are concentrated in Poo block and not in the Nichar block in which study village Sungra is located. Since the Hindus number maximum in Kinnaur, the Hindu traditions and rituals are more prevalent there.

The Kinnauras practise patriarchy. Unlike the north-eastern hill tribes, matriarchy never existed in this part. The property is inherited by the sons. Therefore, it is pertinent to mention, traditionally as well as in the contemporary times, the birth of a son in a family is conceived as an auspicious event. In anticipation of the birth of a son, right from the day of conception, a pregnant woman starts carrying a necklace with a *mantra* inscribed on it by the *Lama* (a Buddhist priest). This practice is observed not among the Buddhists alone but even among Hindus. Some of the Hindu women also bear such a necklace with *mantra* inscribed on it. The *mantra* implies: May God bless the child and the mother! It is a debatable issue as for the putting of necklace by the women is concerned. Is it put on by a woman in anticipation of birth of a son? or is it meant for the well-being of the women bearing a child? Although the *mantra* includes well-being of the mother, but she seems to enjoy this privilege due to the son who needs the mother to nurture him.

This may be substantiated by the fact that a daughter does not have much for her in the family. Even if a daughter lives in the family as unmarried, she does not have any claim over the family property. In real terms, she has no one else to fall back upon. Her difficulties increase after the demise of her parents as she is ordinarily given no share of property by her brothers. Among the girls, the status also depends upon what type of progeny she is. This is important as a distinction is maintained between the legitimate and the illegitimate sons and daughters. The illegitimate son is called *poltu* and does not have any property right. An illegitimate daughter is called *poltee.* She is described as an offspring of adulterous relationship. Since the patriarchy is strong, no one from the father's side takes care of the girl. It is her maternal uncle who takes care of her. This is not a voluntary act of benevolence but a moral obligation which the society expects the maternal uncle to perform. The *poltee* may not be a common phenomenon but it does indicate possible occurrence of certain cases of adultery among Kinnaura women. Whether adultery is a voluntary or an induced act, this is an issue which needs examination in the light of patriarchal value system. It may be that the male who enjoys all rights imposes his will on the helpless woman even against her resistance. This seems to be the most likely case but other reasons cannot be ruled out. To be more conclusive, this aspect needs an exploration. The fact that a separate identity is given to a child born out of adulterous union, therefore, implies that women in general go unheard. This is moreso when the society does not impose any sanction on the male who induces the female or indulges in such an act. Besides the sanctions which the women are subjected to, they have otherwise also to carry on more family responsibilities as mother, wife and keeper of the house in comparison to men.

The historical evidence also suggests social constraints imposed on women which are evolved by the community. Along with the said direct intervention of various rites and rituals in the life of women also affects her work participation. The implication of which is that these religious beliefs certainly render women low in status and restrict them to various types of controls. One such belief rests in the concept of *dain* (witches or evil souls of dead women). With the use of such a concept some women are described "evil-spirited" who by virtue of being evil create troubles for others. What the community does to such women, in the absence of an empirical study is very difficult to say. But it is certain that these women may not be treated as normal human beings and thus may be avoided. At the same time, the exploitation of such women, if enrolled in the labour force, cannot be ruled out.

In contrast to this, one also comes across evidence of Kinnaura women enjoying liberty and freedom. A peep into the life of the Kinnaura, that too from the point of view of traditions and culture, seems to suggest that the only freedom women seem to enjoy is their participation in the social and cultural activities, festivities and other such affairs. This liberty is granted to them because of its functional significance. It is felt that women's free participation in fairs and festivals gives them an opportunity to dress up in their traditional costumes, put on jewelry and make them feel important. The other reason is that such participation provides perfect situations conducive to formation of social relationships. At times, during such festivities young boys and girls find suitable mate for themselves. The other reason may be that their participation is permitted as it provides men some kind of entertainment.

The custom of exchange of heads, is another practice indicating liberty for women. This practice enables a women to have a god brother or a god sister. The relationships, in this way, were considered as good as the blood relation. The woman having such relationships felt assured in themselves to depend upon the "god-brother" or "god-sister" or the person for certain helps in the time of distress. Such type of permissiveness in which the relationships are entirely social and not sexual is perhaps derived from the cult of *devi* (goddess). A *devi* is a pious and divine, wielding lot of *shakti* (power). Therefore, the community also looks at women as a being with power to create. The life of a woman perhaps is like the mother earth which is worshipped for its productive potentials and also used ruthlessly to extract more and more. This is true not of the Kinnauras but women in general. The existence of women, thus remains paradoxical. There are a couple of type of pollution and impurities attached to them during the period of their confinement. Although these restrictions were imposed more from the point of view protection of environment and possible infections but such restrictions affected their work participation, particularly the ones related to household chores, and even to some extent, work participation outside the home. The latter was the case when the women were menstruating. Though it is natural and part of the female biological process, it is often kept secret from others. In this way, one also notices the fact that social, cultural and ritual practices restricted women's participation in work to some extent. In the district gazetteer of Kinnaur, one finds numerous evidences suggesting that women have always been inferior to men with a number of restrictions.

The legitimate way through which sexual unions are established in Kinnaur is marriage, which is solemnised, mostly by Hindus as per the Hindu system of marriage. The marriages, by and large, are monogamous and involve caste and class considerations. Caste and community are very important in such matters. Along with caste, some degree of economic compatibility between the families is also of decisive relevance. In the earlier times, as per the tradition of *rehja*, the marriages were fixed by the parents of the would-be bride and bridegroom at an early age. But these were solemnised at a later age. Polyandrous marriages have been prevalent in Kinnaur for a very long time. Under such marriages, the brothers after their marriage with a girl evolved a system through which they carried out their sexual union without coming in conflict with each other. Moreover, the control of family and the clan was highly assertive. In case of any possible conflict, the family elders intervened in an effective manner.

It is difficult to say what is the extent and incidence of polyandrous unions in Kinnaur. The discussions with the educated Kinnauras seem to suggest that there is a definite decline of polyandry. This type of marriages are found more in the remote areas and that too to a very limited extent. This change is attributed to the increasing value of individualism, induced by education, social and occupational mobility among the younger generations. The educated and the younger age group men and women prefer to go in for monogamous marriages. The elder generation is not averse to change but worry about the possible erosion of family unity and integration in the times to come.

The role of education is increasingly becoming quite crucial but it is not confined only to inducing change in the marriage practices. It, in fact, is becoming a significant aspect of social life of people in Kinnaur. This is, to a large extent, due to the educational development in Himachal Pradesh which in terms of literacy ranks fifth among all the states in India. The other related reason is the occupational mobility among the educated Kinnauras, especially their entry into administrative services in the centre and the state. The evidence (NHFS, 1992) suggests that in the six to ten year age group, the school attendance for males stands at 94 per cent and for females it is 89 per cent. In the 11 to 14 years age group, it is 93 per cent for males and 86 per cent for females. The rural-urban differentials are not profound and are restricted to 6 to 7 per cent. The present state of school attendance is an indication of future rise in the levels of education in the state. This is likely to affect the Kinnauras also. Within Himachal Pradesh, as per the 1991 census, Kinnaur ranked eight among its 12 districts. However, in relation to other tribal areas, i.e., district Lahaul and Spiti, and tehsils Pangi and Bharmour of Chamba district, it even today ranks first. Since women education has received considerable attention, 42.04 per cent of the total women in Kinnaur are literate including those who are educated at varying levels. The majority of the educated women are in the younger age group. However, in comparison to female education in non-tribal districts, the literacy among women in Kinnaur continues to be low.

The evidence collected from the study area also substantiates that education among the Kinnaura women is picking up in the district and indicates encouraging trends. Table 3.1 shows that only one-fifth of the women interviewed are illiterate. The remaining 80.3 per cent are literate with varying levels of formal education. Among the educated, 15.3 per cent have primary school education, 31.1 per cent have gone up to the middle school, and 31.3 per cent have passed high school. The number of women having education beyond high school is very limited.

Table 3.1

Education-wise Distribution

Educational Level	*Frequency*	*Percentage*
Illiterate	77	19.7
Primary	60	15.3
Middle	118	30.1
High School	123	31.3
B.A.	13	3.3
M.A.	1	.3
Total	392	100.0

The trend indicates that after middle school the number of women in education starts declining. It, thus, indicates that a very limited number go in for higher education. However, the overall trend of education based on the number of women included in the sample indicates that in Kinnaur the literacy among women is higher than the state and national literacy level. It is, however, difficult to spell out the reasons for higher literacy in this village. The only possible reason can be the maximum number of women the younger age group in the sample of the present study*. It has been stated earlier that the education among the younger age group females is higher in comparison to that of those who are in the higher age group.

* Age group (in years): up to 20 = 13.5%, 21-25 = 29.3%, 26-30 = 23.5%, 31-35 = 19.9%, 36-40 = 12.8%, 41+ = 1.0%.

Table 3.2
Major Occupations of Respondents

Occupation	*Frequency*	*Percentage*
House wife	9	2.3
Housewife and agriculture	377	96.2
Government service	6	1.5
Total	392	100.0

Women in Kinnaur, like other parts of the country, have been economically dependent on men. However, their contribution to the family economy, if not more has probably been equal to that of men. It is obvious from Table 3.2 that in addition to their household chores, they participate in agricultural operations to a considerable extent. In accordance with the Kinnaura tradition, the women do not till the land as they are customarily forbidden to do so. The reason cited by men in general is that ploughing requires use of force, which is associated with men. If the women are asked to do this type of work, it is something derogatory for men. Interestingly, tilling of land is equated with women fertility in which the role of man is to sow the seed and the role of woman like the earth is to produce. In other agricultural activities, the women remain very important contributors.

Despite their significant role in the process of production, which is basic to the fulfillment of human needs, women, by and large, remain deprived of property rights. It is only recently that a very few sensitised women, who are educated and are engaged in some occupations outside home, particularly those in the government organisations have started making claims to property as their right. The constitutional privileges extended to scheduled tribes are mostly utilised by the Kinnaura men. This benefit is also now being enjoyed by women to a limited extent. Consequently, they are entering the organised sector or government jobs. In the sample of the present study, the number of such women is just 1.5 per cent. Out of these six women, one is in Class II category occupation and others are in Class III category. The lesser involvement of women in occupations outside home, i.e., in the government jobs, and their maximum concentration in agriculture and related work is conditioned by their low educational accomplishments. At the same time, it is here desirable to mention that there are some women with graduation degree in the sample of the study. The women's march towards higher education, of course, can be judged from the good number of Kinnaura girls pursuing postgraduate courses in universities. The spirit of competition among them is being instilled in the changing social scenario as some of them even prepare for competitive examinations. A large number of women in the study sample, however, either due to certain family or because of non-availability of job are not working in the organised sector. The sector of employment of women in the case of majority of the respondents is unorganised "self-employed" category. Their number in the unorganised private sector is also not very large. Only 0.5 per cent of them have taken up employment in private sector, that is, working in private unorganised sector which also includes seasonal working on other's agricultural lands and/or engaging in some construction work.

It was noted in the foregoing paragraph that the women in accordance with traditions and culture of Kinnaur did not have any property rights. Moreover, most of them being working on their own agricultural land, the value of their labour was never calculated in economic terms. Therefore, they are supposed to have no income of their own. This is the logical fallout of the fact that the work done by women is not considered of any economic value. The trend seems to be changing as the women claim of having an income of their own. Such disclosures by women were difficult to come about due to general inhibitions among them. It is also a fact that the problem extracting information from respondents, particularly the women is widely confronted during the course of collection of data not only about income but also other aspects of the study. However, the income stated by the respondents was taken at its face value and was recorded as it is. Some attempts to probe into their claim resulted in no further information. It was, therefore, not probed much.

Table 3.3
Income-wise Distribution

Income per Month (in Rs.)	*Frequency*	*Percentage*
No income	278	70.9
Up to 1,000	100	25.5
1,001-2,000	5	1.3
3,000-4,000	5	1.4
4,001-5,000	4	0.8
Total	392	100.0

The income-wise classification of the respondents presented in Table 3.3 indicates that majority of the respondents (70.9%) do not have any income. Among those who have an income up to Rs. 1,000 per month constitute 25.5 per cent of the total sample. The remaining 1.3 per cent earn an income between Rs. 1,001-2,000, 1.4 per cent between Rs. 3,000-4,000 and only 0.8 per cent are placed in the income range of Rs. 4,001-5,000 per month. On the basis of the income distribution pattern it is obvious that majority of the women in the sample fall in the below poverty line income group. This is largely true of women at large. However, the ranking within these varying income levels indicates that majority of the respondents fall in the low income group and a negligible minority falls in the middle and high income groups.

The status of married women in Indian society in general and the Kinnauras in particular is not independent but dependent on their husbands. Since the present study intends to examine fertility behaviour, it also takes into consideration the demographic and socio-economic attributes of the husbands of the respondents.

Table 3.4

Age-wise Distribution of Husbands

Age Group (in years)	*Frequency*	*Percentage*
Up to 25	8	2.0
26-30	61	15.6
31-35	110	28.1
36-40	82	20.9
41-45	80	20.4
46-50	44	11.2
51 and above	7	1.8
Total	392	100.0

Table 3.4 indicates that maximum of the respondents' (28.1%) fall in the 31-35 years age group and other 20.9 per cent and 20.4 per cent fall in the 36-40 and 41-45 years age group respectively. The number of husbands falling in the 46-50 year age group and 51+ years and above is constituted by 11.2 per cent and 1.8 per cent respectively. In comparison to the age structure of the respondents, the husbands are in relatively higher age groups. This is because of the general socio-cultural practices of

Indian society due to which women at the time of their marriage are generally younger to their husbands.

Table 3.5
Education-wise Distribution of Husbands

Husbands' Education	*Frequency*	*Percentage*
Illiterate	18	4.6
Literate	3	.8
Primary	15	3.8
Middle	87	22.2
High School	194	49.5
B.A./B.Sc.	66	16.8
M.A./M.Sc.	9	2.3
Total	392	100.0

The data presented in Table 3.5 indicate that the husbands have relatively higher level of formal education than their counterparts. While in the illiterate category there were 19.4 per cent women. In comparison to them, only 4.6 per cent of the husbands are illiterate. Similarly, in other categories the number of the husbands is quite high. The difference is particularly visible in the primary, middle and high school education categories. The same is also true in the case of those having education upto other higher levels. In the primary school category, the number of husbands is just 3.8 per cent. In the middle school, it is 22.2 per cent and in high school it is 49.5 per cent.

The higher levels of education of the husbands shows the gender bias in educating the girl child which prevailed in the past. This bias is likely to be reflected for some more time due to the patriarchal nature of Kinnaur society and relatively more attention given to the education of the male child. This is also one of the reasons why in Kinnaur as a whole 72.04 per cent of the total males are literate and in comparison to them only 42.04 per cent women fall in the literate category.

Table 3.6

Occupation-wise Distribution of Husbands

Husbands' Occupation	*Frequency*	*Percentage*
Agriculture	188	48.0
Government service (Class III & IV)	139	35.4
Shopkeeper	55	14.1
Carpenter/blacksmith	10	2.5
Total	392	100.0

The occupational classification of husbands presented in Table 3.6 indicates that despite their relatively higher educational level 48 per cent of them are engaged in agricultural activities. However, in comparison to them, 35.4 per cent of the husbands are in government service, occupying Class III and IV positions. Some of them also run small-scale business, which is largely confined to a small time grocery or other general merchant shop. Only 2.5 per cent are working as carpenters and blacksmiths. Unlike other areas where carpentry and smithy have been caste specific occupations, in Kinnaur such occupations are also carried out by scheduled castes who acquire some vocational training in some of these trades. In comparison to data in Table 3.2, it is quite evident that more women work in the agricultural fields than their husbands. This is partly due to the fact that most of the families in general have small agricultural holdings, the wives looks after that and the husbands with higher educational level find out some work elsewhere away from home or start with some small business depending upon his economic capability.

The question regarding the household income was also put to the respondents. Like the women's reluctance in informing about their own income, they were hesitant in telling about the total income of their household. The household-wise distribution of the income enumerated in Table 3.7 is as it was told by the respondents themselves. Since this is a very sensitive area of information and the people belonging to scheduled tribes are also beneficiary of various schemes and benefits from the government, they also fear giving a true picture of the household income and therefore, such an information does not come handy.

Table 3.7
Household Income

Household Income (in Rs. per month)	*Frequency*	*Percentage*
Up to 1,000	52	13.3
1,001-2,000	158	40.3
2,001-3,000	115	29.3
3,001-4,000	54	13.8
4,001-5,000	1	.3
5,001-6,000	12	3.1
Total	392	100.0

Data on household income indicate that maximum of them (40.3%) have an income ranging between Rs. 1,001-2,000 per month. This, therefore, means that a good number of respondents are in the range of double the poverty-line limit. This concept of double the poverty-line is used in Himachal Pradesh government departments who adopt it in identifying the poor people for the grant of loans. In other income categories, i.e., Rs. 2,001-3,000 and Rs. 3,001-4,000 there are 29.3 per cent and 13.8 per cent households respectively. Beyond Rs. 4,001 income the number of the households is just 3.4 per cent. This is indicative of the general pattern of income distribution in Himachal Pradesh as a whole. Although the claim of the state is that the number of the people below poverty-line has declined but the per capita income in Himachal Pradesh is just Rs. 7,784 per annum which is below the poverty-line income of Rs. 11,000 per annum declared by the government itself. In general, the larger number of the people have less income and smaller number of people have more income. As stated earlier, it may be noted that during the empirical exercise the respondents were found to hide their actual income due to the fears well known to them.

Women's Work Participation and Decision-Making

In the previous section, it was observed that the women in majority number take part in the agricultural operations, and thus supplement their household income by way of adding to the agricultural production. In the majority cases, it is also noted that their participation in agriculture is in addition to their traditional household chores. It is a known fact that women's participation in work outside the four walls of their home is conditioned by the regional needs and cultural factors to a significant extent. At the same time, the role of economic pressures and compulsions of the family in sending the women out to work cannot be undermined. A good number of studies conducted on women's participation in the workforce in developing countries acknowledge this fact.

Most of the working women in the developing economies

are found engaged in agricultural work (Freedman and Wai, 1988). The nature of work done by them in the agricultural fields includes the pre and post-harvest operations as well as vegetable gardening. A good number of rural women raise animals. In Pakistan, approximately 73 per cent of women belonging to agricultural households work in the labour force. Among them 54 per cent are engaged mainly in agricultural work on their family farms. Another 16 per cent working in non-agriculture activities are in the non-family farms, 3 per cent are employed elsewhere (United Nations, 1993). This is comparable even with the case of Kinnaur where women are doing agricultural labour but mostly on their own farms. Similarly, women's participation in the labour force is fast increasing in developing countries like Mexico. On the basis of Mexican experience, one may say that in a poor country, the general educational level of women is low. Therefore, most of these women are likely to participate in the low prestige occupations (United Nations, 1993: 35-38).

It is also observed that in many other studies women's work participation outside their home has increased due to increasing urbanisation and industrialisation. The evidence suggests that the operation of these forces have provided sufficient impetus to women's work participation in the monetarily beneficial activities. Even when the work wages remain low for most of these women, their participation in workforce helps them in increasing the total household income.

Dixon (1982) points out that in developing countries most of the women work in the informal sector and they carry on unpaid work in the agricultural farms. In addition, it is further noted that a large number of women in general occupy low social status. The economic needs of the household are, very often, the most compelling reasons for these women to work

(United Nations, 1985). Why did women not work in the earlier times and why do they work these days can be explained in a comparative perspective. It is a common place observation that lifestyle in the developing countries are changing fast and heading more towards consumerism. This has led to rising pressures on the household economy. Even higher level of fertility and rising inflation and prices in the developing nations have caused a need for further mobilisation of resources.

It is pertinent to mention that the levels of women's work participation depend on the level of development of the society concerned. The theory of demographic transition becomes relevant here as this may have direct and indirect relationship between, not only development induced work participation but also its possible influences on fertility behaviour. The thrust of this theory is that the level of economic development acts as an effective instrument in increasing economic activities and this results in bringing down the level of fertility. The underlying assumption here being that increase in the number of economic activities is likely to provide more and more work opportunities and employment avenues to women. While their increased participation in work is important *vis-à-vis* generating income to meet family needs, the impact of it on fertility depends a great deal on a number of other factors which mediate between population growth and levels of development (Mueller and Tabah, 1975).

There are two juxtaposed experiences which point out that the demographic transition theory does not always operate in the expected manner. The experience of some countries show that some of the developed counties witnessed reduction in fertility during the period of great economic depression and baby boon after the World War II when these societies picked up development. Similarly, it also becomes a problem to understand why a country like Cuba experienced increase in birth rate after revolution in 1960 when it also had economic development. Such situations explain that economic development does not always negative population growth. At times, development needs boost population growth through immigration of labour which the economic development process of that particular country needs. It is in this way that development *per se* is not the only factor determining fertility. May be the labour need of the growing economy has its own dynamics. Therefore, one needs to understand fertility rather more minutely and in relation to other factors. The problem is also confronted in understanding why Cuba had decreased birth rate in the face of economic deterioration. While this indicates that the use of income criteria in measuring women's work participation remains defiance it also brings about certain problems in the decision-making process which, in all probability, seems to be associated with women's economic power (also see D'Souza, 1983; Sharma, 1995).

There is an alternate explanation which suggests that it is not the income but the economic adjustment which the working and non-working women make in relation to number of children they may like to have. This economic adjustment, argues D'Souza (1983) effects the decision-making with regard to the number of children a family wishes to have. Through this argument D'Souza tries to suggest that the economic situation of the couple concerned is subject to change with their upward and/or downward mobility. In fact, it is the social mobility of the individuals which plays an important role in affecting the attitudes, behaviour and decision-making process with regard to birth of child in the family.

The concept of economic adjustment used by D'Souza states that economic development or its index is replaced by sectional and occupational transformation. In addition to the said, it is further argued by him that replacement of economic development by other variables also helps the individual in the identification of the number of opportunity for employment available in the social structure and the degree to which these have been exploited by the people will influence the chance of reduction in birth rate. The logic of the argument is that with economic development and expansion of the non-agricultural employment sector human being's dependence decreases on the primary sector of economy. The new opportunities induce conditions far spatial as well as social mobility. Since these differences are visible at the micro and the macro-level and also at the inter-generation level, the fertility differentials also become significant when analysed in the light of such parameters. It is, therefore, hypothesised that the women who participate in the work have significant say in the social, economic and family related decisions. The possible empowerment of women which takes place through such a process, probably also effects decisions of the women with regard to bearing or not bearing of additional children.

It may be recalled that in the beginning of the chapter it was also hypothesised that the relationship between work participation and decision-making and its subsequent effect on the decisions regarding fertility is governed by certain specific conditions which emanate from the social and cultural setting in which one is placed. How far the above assumptions apply to the situation in Kinnaur is examined in the light of empirical data. Following the foregoing discussion this chapter tends to examine the availability of work opportunities to the women in the study area and the nature of women's work participation, and their say in the decision making processes.

The work participation of women depends upon their social status in the society, i.e., their education, socio-cultural values attached with the work they do and availability of work

Table 3.8
Employment Opportunities

Employment	*Frequency*	*Percentage*
No response	1	.3
Agriculture	48	12.2
Horticulture	54	13.8
Road constructor	286	73.0
Handloom/handicraft	3	.8
Total	392	100.0

in the vicinity of their living. In the context of Kinnaur, the work opportunities are not very many as the entire district has not undergone industrial development or administrative expansion. Therefore, the types of jobs known to the women are in the labour force as road construction workers, weavers on handlooms, handicraft artisans and in agriculture and horticulture. Although these women mainly work in agriculture sector yet majority among them (73%) indicate that work on road is generally available to them as can be seen from Table 3.8. One of the reasons perhaps is that due to repair work of the roads, such type of work goes on for a considerable period of time in a year. The industrial activities are very limited. In fact, the only industrial development or the project which provides job opportunities to local people and mentioned by women is power project in their area, particularly Bhabha Hydel Electric Power Project located at Sungra. The project, however, does not have much to offer to women. But the men from the area do get employment in the project at various levels. By and large, they do labour work.

Table 3.9 indicates that the distance of location of the place where work opportunities are available to the respondents ranges between less than a km to more than 5 km For majority of the people (59.2%) these opportunities are available within a radius of 5 km. The majority, however, is living within a distance of about 4 to 5 km.

Table 3.9

Distance of Location of Employment Opportunities

Distance	*Frequency*	*Percentage*
Less than 1 km	1	.3
1 km	44	11.2
2 km	73	18.6
4 km	41	10.5
5 km	232	59.2
Total	392	100.0

One tendency which is emerging among people of Kinnaur is that some of the male members migrate to places away from their homes for the purpose of employment. This is confirmed by 40.6 per cent of the respondents who have one or the other member of their family living at some other place away from home. The implication of such a movement of the male population is some degree of occupational diversification, spatial as well as social mobility. But their movement restricts the women to look after their agriculture. They, therefore, are not able to move away to other places for work. In the given background of low educational profile, family constraints and other obligations they have to contend with the locally available employment opportunities. Unlike men, their twin role of keeper of the family and supplementing family income by working on their own agricultural or horticultural land restrict their mobility within the boundaries of the village.

Table 3.10
Nature of Work Participation

Work Participation	*Frequency*	*Percentage*
Government service	6	1.6
Household, agriculture and horticulture	374	95.4
Household, agriculture and road construction	12	3.1
Total	392	100.0

Table 3.10 indicates that majority of women are involved in the household, agricultural and horticultural activities. These women account for 95.4 per cent of total sample. Although no woman stated that she worked as a construction labourer when the question about their occupation was asked but 3.1 per cent women while discussing about the nature and type of their employment revealed that they at times carry on activities which are not at all done by them as per their family tradition. To work as road construction labour and construction labour by women is not a preferred occupation.

Table 3.11
Average Hours of Household Work

Hours of Work	*Frequency*	*Percentage*
5	216	55.1
6	162	41.3
8+	14	3.6
Total	392	100.0

The question regarding the number of hours they put in carrying out their household chores and other than household activities revealed that most women were doing very hard work. The data furnished in Table 3.11 indicate that 55.1 per cent women, on an average spend five hours in household activities and 41.3 per cent women spend six hours in meeting their household needs. The number of women spending more than eight hours is only 3.6 per cent. Spending of time in the household activities does not mean end of the day for them and they retire to bed. The remaining time they utilise for other income supplementing activities.

Table 3.12

Average Hours of Work other than Household

Hours of Work	*Frequency*	*Percentage*
Not Applicable	9	2.3
3	75	17.8
4	215	54.8
5	93	23.7
6+	9	2.3
Total	392	100.0

In comparison to data in Table 3.11, the data in Table 3.12 indicate that in addition to their household work 54.8 per cent of the women spend on an average four hours in other than household activities. This is followed by 23.7 and 2.3 per cent women who spend five and six hours respectively in other than household activities. The number of women spending around three hours in such activities is 17.8 per cent. In this way, the women in Kinnaur are doubly burdened. The intensity and magnitude of their work vary in terms of the number of hours spent by them in carrying out their household and non-household work. There are only 2.3 per cent women who do not do anything other than their household work.

One of the paradoxes of women's life is that they are required to work but their work does not get any appreciation. This is also true of the Kinnaura women. In the study sample, 54.3 per cent of the women complained that they do not get any appreciation for the work they do for their family. It is simply considered as their moral obligation to work for the family. On the other hand, 45.7 per cent women find some appreciation of their work by their men. It may, however, be noted that despite non-appreciating attitudes of men towards women's work outside the home, the women continue to carry on such activities to make the family comfortable. It is also stated by the women that it is not as per their own wish that they work in the fields. It is because there is no alternative for them.

What to talk of men's attitude, the attitude of women themselves towards working of women outside their home indicates some kind of cynicism and pessimism. The argument the women tender to this effect is that it is not by choice but because of economic needs of the family that they have to work. They put in considerable hard work for the family. But, in the absence of any reward, even if they work outside the home it is not without reservations. Therefore, a majority of women argues that what is important is that the women, instead of their exploitation in the process of need fulfillment, should make the men realise that women's work is as important as theirs. What they mean by this is that the recognition of their work should itself be forthcoming from the members of their families. This they feel can be done only by organising the women against injustice to them.

The data with regard to women's occupation, their work participation and the attitudes of men and women towards their work have been quite revealing in two ways. First, almost all women in the sample are found participating in work irrespective of existing attitudes of men and women. Second, the women themselves also have certain reservations about their working outside home. These reservations, particularly arise due to the duality which they observe in the behaviour of men. On the one hand, the men want them to work, on the other the same men are also critical of their working. Do women's work participation outside home and the contribution they make towards the family income enables them to have a say in the decision-making in the family, i.e., in the social, economic and family related---number of children they have or should have, decisions.

Table 3.13

Participation in Major Social and Economic and Size of Family Related Decisions

Participation	*Frequency*	*Percentage*
Self	20	5.1
Husband	333	84.9
Parents-in-law	39	9.9
Total	392	100.0

According to Table 3.13, contrary to the expectations that work participation enables the women to take important decisions, only 5.1 per cent of the women in the study sample are found involved in the decision-making processes and accordingly take major social and economic decisions of the family. In the case of 84.9 per cent all important social, economic and other family related major decisions are made by their husbands. Since parents-in-law also live with some of the respondents, 9.9 per cent of the women also stated that their parents-in-law often intervene in the family matters and therefore, they have more say in the decision-making process. Their husbands cannot deny the decisions made by them as among the Kinnauras patriarchy as well as group sentiments are very strong.

It is also reported that in case a dispute arises in a family, then at times it is referred to the clan *devta*. Because of the fears that others would come to know about the family dispute, the interference and interventions of the family elders are often respected. It is very rare that a decision made by the elders is defied by the younger members of the family. One of the reasons also being that invariably people of Kinnaur have some amount of family land. This, under the law of inheritance, is transferred to the next generation. In case of inter-generation conflict, the fear of excommunication also makes the younger generations to accept the elders' words. From this, it appears that despite women's involvement in economically gainful activities, they do not have much say in the economic as well as social affairs of the family. The socio-economic identification of those who stated that they themselves take the decisions, reveals that six of them employed in government jobs with relatively higher education and income of their own. The others enjoy this status because of their own education. This, therefore, implies that work participation *per se* does not enable an individual to affect decisions in the family. Along with work participation, the nature of employment, income levels, the extent of the economic contribution the woman makes to the family assets and level of education are also very significant.

The argument about decision-making was further extended to the area of bearing of children. The inquiry made in this regard revealed the similar trends. The respondents in majority (94.9%) told that, by and large, the decisions regarding the number of children the family should have are not exactly consciously affected by anyone in the family. But their husbands and their parents-in-law do prevail over. A woman remarked that it is basically the social pressures or the expectation of the community which are reflected through their husbands and they go in for additional child. Generally, opinions of the women do not matter.

To sum up, the foregoing descriptive analysis and discussion of the socio-cultural, demographic and economic profile of the women in general and the respondents, their work participation and involvement in the family decision-making process, the following findings are obvious. It is found that majority of women in the sample of the study falls in the highly reproductive age group. There are women who are beyond 40 years of age, but their number is very small. The women, except for a very few cases belong to Hindu religion. The caste categorisation reveals two major caste groups, namely, high caste and scheduled castes. The high caste is represented mainly by the Rajputs. In this way, these characteristics of the respondents also reflect on the nature and type of social structure of Kinnaur where Hindus are in preponderance. Although designated as tribe, social structure of Kinnaur is almost same as that of the Indian society at large. In other words, there is a socially structured caste hierarchy which further legitimises the caste hierarchy. With regard to women's work participation and their say in the decision-making process of the family, it is found that the nature of work of majority of the women is manual as they have to work in the fields as well as carry on the household chores. Although educational profile indicates that a good number of respondents are educated but their number in the formal sector of employment is highly negligible. This is because of the fact that most of these women seem to get married at a young age which prevents them from going for a vocation. Also, the addition of family responsibilities further puts limits on their chances of getting employment. The other factors responsible for lesser number of women in formal sector is the agriculture and horticultural activities which as part of family responsibilities they have to carry on for supplementing their household income. Moreover, the job opportunities are also scarce in the area. Being married and with children, these women cannot afford to go to far off places to take up employment.

The data with regard to their participation in the household, agriculture and horticulture work make the life of these women highly burdened. The Kinnaura women, on an average work for as many as 8 to 12 hours a day. While these women work to supplement their household income, their work does not carry any recognition by their menfolk. More than 50 per cent of the women carry this feeling that their work is not appreciated. It is, therefore, quite obvious that despite the fact that women work much more than the men their contribution is not recognised. They, therefore, do not enjoy high social status. What to talk of high status, they do not have a status even equal to that of men. Their say in the major decision-making process of the family is also negligible. The data indicate that the major social and economic decisions are taken by the men. More than the respondents is the say of their parents-in-law in the family affairs. The latter enjoy autonomy because of their age as well as the patriarchal nature of Kinnaura society. In this way, this chapter points out that in the rural areas with its specific socio-cultural setting the women work participation does not necessarily enables them to participate in the decision-making process in an effective manner and nor it adds to their empowerment at the level of the family.

4 Child Bearing and Contraception

The previous two chapters dealt with the social, cultural and economic dimensions of women's status, their participation in work outside home and their involvement in the decision-making process of the family. It has been observed that the existential conditions of women in Kinnaur, like the women in other parts of Indian society, are not conducive to their development. The social constraints limit their movements and also make them rare and ineffective participant in the decision-making process in the family. In the discussion of theoretical and methodological issues, it has also been assumed that fertility behaviour is largely influenced by the social structure. The underlying assumption here being that marriage practices and the kind of sexual unions a society permits have definite linkages with fertility. Different societies have a set of values governing marriages. In India, the purpose of marriage is to have progeny, and the emphasis is laid down on begetting a son. Such values are found to have a determining effect on child bearing practices. The official norms regarding the number of children may be in conflict with the community norms governing the size of the family and therefore, may interfere in the process of adoption of family planning practices in a society. Logically, such a conflict of values may also affect whether to or not to adopt family planning devices. In this way, social structure seems to affect the family planning practices. Since, both marriage and family planning practices being significant in fertility behaviour, this chapter attempts at analysing the prevalent marriage, family planning and child bearing practices in the social-structural context of Kinnaur.

Marriage Practices in Kinnaur

The institution of marriage is universal but exists in diverse forms and types. Accordingly, people solemnise marriages in different ways and manners. How far diversity in marriage practices influences differential fertility is not known basically due to the paucity of empirical data and studies. However, some aspects of marriage practices, such as age at marriage, duration of marriage and its termination are reported to have some degree of relationship with fertility behaviour. The studies conducted in 1960s and early 1970s in India and abroad indicate a lower fertility for those women who marry at a higher age in comparison to those who get married at a relatively younger age (United Nations, 1961; Driver, 1963; Agrawala, 1962; Mukherjee, 1962; Jan, 1964; Jhan and Garden, 1971). The same trend continues to be associated with general fertility patterns even in the 1980s and 1990s.

The institution of marriage, as per its traditionally defined functions, establishes a family, the smallest social unit of the society, carries on reproduction, and provides continuity to the society. With its well-defined rules the institution of marriage regulates sexual behaviour of the members. Radcliffe-Brown and Malinowski, by keeping in view such functions argue that marriage and family thus prevent possible chaos in the social relationships. Reproduction, although a biological process, is also a social and cultural phenomenon. The social and cultural aspects regulate sexual life of the couples through a structure of values. One way to understand this relationship is possible through an examination of a society attaching value to polygamous and monogamous type marriages. The risk of fertility certainly increases in the former type of marriages. Radcliffe-Brown, considering marriage as a cultural phenomenon, argues that in a polygamous society, particularly the polyandrous ones in which sharing of the wife by co-husbands is culturally acceptable, the risk of pregnancies is possibly higher than those societies practicing monogamous marriages. In polygamous system---polyandry and polygyny---the society makes arrangements not only to maintain the large number of husbands and wives respectively but also provides support to children born out of such unions. In case the belief that women have a natural instinct to become mothers and it is accepted, the possibility of high fertility will always be there even when the social values do not approve of large number of children.

In a monogamous society, the marriage symbolises more responsibility with relative autonomous identity of the spouse. In such a system, although the couple bears joint responsibility of bearing and rearing children, but due to patriarchy it is the woman who has to do much more in comparison to a man. Similarly, the trends seem to suggest that the couples due to nuclearisation of family are found to have differential levels of fertility in such societies. The etiology suggests that varying levels of fertility are caused by many other factors such as the age at marriage, the length of marital union, the frequency of coitus, and the values attached with coitus. Davis and Blake (1968) referred to as many as 11 intervening factors. They argue that the role of institutional arrangements is very vital as it is found directly affecting fertility behaviour. One also needs to have a critical view of the underlying conditions which result in varying type of marriages and the associated practices in different societies. Goode (1963) with reference to different societies argue that the emergence of monogamy as a form of marriage is the consequence of freedom, liberty, modernisation and the emerging way of life, such as urban, industrial and the processes associated with these ways. In fact, from Goode's sociological point of view the transformation of family from polygamous to nuclear has been widely considered as a result of social evolution of the society, particularly the new patterns of social relationships which emerged in the 1960s and 1970s. Clifford (1971), Davis and Moore (1969), Wyon and Gorden (1971) and Stycos (1967) analysed the then changes in marriage patterns and fertility from the point of view of modernisation. The modernisation thesis, therefore, also included its concomitant processes such as urbanisation, industrialisation and higher level of rationalisation in a society. Thereby indicating that the new values given by these processes also affect fertility among different groups.

In view of the foregoing discussion of sociological and anthropological views about the marriage, family and to some extent their relation with fertility it is expected that marriage practices and associated factors have a significant role in the regulation of fertility behaviour. The rationale underlying this assumption is that the living arrangements of marricd couples with and without procreation are regulated through several intermediary variables. These in turn are also affected by the nature and type of marriage practices (Agrawala, 1967; Bumpass, 1969; Goldberg, 1959; Kim, 1965; Kirk, 1968; Lorimer, et al., 1954; Mitchel, 1971; Rele et al., 1972).

Before analysing the empirical data, it is imperative to mention that in the Indian society institution of marriage, having traces of its origin in the Hindu texts, is very significant with regard to fertility behaviour. According to the indological perspective the union between a male and a female is a sacred affair and not merely a mean of sex need gratification. Although at present, marriage is a universal institution but the mode and manner of its solemnisation and social recognition is not universal. The nature, type, practice and associated rituals of marriage differ from society to society. The aim of marriage according to Hindu philosophy is fulfillment of *dharma* (religious obligation), *praja* (progeny), and *kama* (sex). Traditionally, it is believed that around 450 A.D. the *tantric* ideas and philosophy was in vogue. It offered two-fold objectives. First, *bhakti* (some type of sacred enjoyment) and second *mukti* (the final liberation from the birth and death cycle). In this respect, no discrimination based on caste, race, tribe and sex was made. In this way, one mode of rituals accorded religious status to marital unions and which helped men and women to get liberation from the cycle of births, re-births and deaths. At the same time, it also implied that the union between men and women and their sex relationships were governed by certain religious prescriptions. In Hinduism, gratification of personal physical or sex needs is not the only goal of marriage but it is a medium to attain certain ends an individual is expected to achieve. This is also evident from the fact of last place assigned to *kama* which clearly indicates that it is not considered as the sole guiding rule of life. Marriage in the Indian setting is more of a social and religious obligation as its main purpose is observing one's *dharma* through the perpetuation of the institution of family as well as the continuance of the group through progeny (Kapadia, 1966: 30). It, therefore, not only becomes a social union but also a 'holy union' between a man and a woman far begetting progeny, particularly a son. It is a necessity for the attainment of salvation and for the fulfillment of religious duties. Besides, a

Hindu marriage is permanent in nature as it is not considered as dissolved even after the death of anyone of the partners. Kapadia further observes that marriage added a social duty towards the family and the community. The individual interests did matter but only a little. It is considered sacred because it becomes complete only with the performance of sacred rites as per the prescribed sacred or ritual systems (Kapadia, 1966: 168).

It may, however, be noted that at some initial stage of the development of human society the relationship between a man and a woman in Indian society must have been more of a promiscuous type. But such a contention is not supported by the early Vedic literature. There is no evidence to suggest that the relations between the sexes were promiscuous and unregulated (Kane, 1941). It is also imperative to mention here that Indian history is generally traced from the Aryans. The Rig Vedic period literature suggests that during that period the Aryans had already developed certain code to regulate their sexual life. However, the code of conduct, under certain conditions of helplessness could be relaxed and therefore, was somewhat permissive. It allowed practice of *niyoga* (sex with other man than the husband) in case the woman was not able to bear a child from her husband. Since begetting progeny was associated with religious obligations of marriage *niyoga* was considered as a sacred act.

In the contemporary times, Indian society does not constitute a homogeneous unit. The same could also be true of the earlier times as the rites and rituals were not observed in a uniform manner all over the country. It had wide variations in terms of caste, cultural and linguistic groups and communities. The same continues but in a more diversified way in the contemporary times. Each one has an elaborate system of marriage, values and meaning attached with martial unions. A number of studies conducted on India's tribal marriage practices suggest different forms of procuring a bride. However, with the general process of social change certain degree of aberrations are also taking place, particularly in the case of those tribal areas which have undergone modernisation in terms of educational advancement, occupational diversification and social as well as spatial mobility. It has been, thus, found that even among some of the tribal communities who have their own social system, culture and norms there exits a tendency to follow the dominant culture and practices of Hindu society or the prevalent Brahmanical values. It is no surprise to find some of the tribal people following the Hindu marriage practices. The *metis* of Manipur is one of the examples, who have over the years become Hindus. This could also be true of some of the tribes, particularly the Kinnauras who directly or indirectly follow Hindu social practices in majority.

What follows from the above is that, by and large, in India as well as in other societies of the world, the institutional regularisation of the relationship between men and women has essentially taken four forms, namely, monogamy, polygamy, polyandry and group marriage. But each type of marriage has either different connotations or has been practised differently in different societies. Monogamy, the simplest form of marriage and most popular in the contemporary times as well as in the past, has been nearly universal in nature. It consists of one male and one female united through the bonds of marriage and endures for the culturally prescribed period such as the life time of at least one of the partners. At the same time, it makes a singular, monolithic form of marriage. It prevails in a variety of forms. For instance, it can be found as a marriage lasting a life time of a partner spanning over eternity. Barnard (1956) in the western context described social monogamy as a permanent form of marriage in which a series of marital partners can be secured by a man or woman. But, at one time, only one partner lives as a legal husband. If a spouse dies or a divorce takes place, such events do not merely indicate the termination of a monogamous marriage. In such events, the partners may have another monogamous marriage and continue to have marital relationship.

Indian society, on the contrary, represents monogamous marriage as the one spanning over eternity. The practice of *sati* symbolised the inseparability of married couples even when death occurred. In the *Dharamshastras* and the *Smritis*, mutual fidelity was attached greater importance. Manu declared mutual fidelity till death as the essence of *dharma* for the husband and the wife. According to him, men and women united in marriage, should constantly so assist themselves in such a way that they may not be disunited and may not violate their mutual fidelity (Kapadia, 1966: 181). This type of a marriage is made permanent by many other ideals and myths, such as *pativaratya* (religiously devoted to one's husband). These ideals and practices, as the history suggests have stood as guards against second marriage or divorce in the Hindu social set-up. At the same time, it is also important to remember that these ideals operated in the framework of patriarchy and thus provided social sanctions against the practice of hypergamy.

Polygamy, the second most common form of marriage around the world, is opposite to the third form of marriage, i.e., polyandry. Polygamy refers to marriage of a male with two or more females. The other form of polygamous marriages is polyandry under which a female marries two or more persons, preferably the brothers. This is called fraternal polyandry. Do different forms of polygamy lead to fertility differentials? It has been noted earlier that polygamy is expected to provide a man opportunity to enter into legitimate marital relationship with different women. In the case of such marriages the possibility of different women bearing children from the same man simultaneously also increases. Since this form of marriage has been a part of the royal families and the elite sections of the society, the evidence of a number of claimants as King's progeny suggests that they had large number of children who were settled by way of recruitment in royal offices, army or by way of allotting them a piece of land. The Hindu texts permitted polygamy in case one wife was unable to bear a male child. At this juncture, it may be mentioned that higher value attached with a male child in the Hindu society even in the modern times reflects on its association with high fertility (Mahadevan, 1979: 65-72).

Polyandry, the other form of polygamy, is practised among the Todan and Tiyans of southern India and the Khusa of the sub-Himalayan region in north India. It is also found among tribes and castes which are patrilineal (Kapadia, 1966: 84). In Himachal Pradesh, polyandrous marriages at one time quite prevalent, have been confined to some part of the upper hills especially Kinnaur, Lahul and Spiti, and Chamba districts. It has also been practiced even in Sirmour district, especially among the groups notified as tribal. However, over the years there has been a considerable change in this regard, particularly due to emergence of individualism, nuclearisation of the family and the households.

At the official level, i.e., under the provisions of Hindu Marriage Act of 1955 and the later amendments, monogamy is the only acceptable form of marriage. But in some remote areas of Kinnaur polyandry does exist. This may be called polyandry in the hidden form.

In the light of the foregoing brief discussion of marriage practices followed in India in general and also in some tribal areas in particular, there are two questions which have been explored in the field setting and presented here with the empirical data. First, what type of marriage practices prevail in the contemporary Kinnaur? Second, how far different types of marriage practices influence fertility behaviour or what relationship these have with the fertility behaviour? With regard to the second question it is too difficult to say as there is hardly any evidence reflecting on the relationship between type of marriage and fertility behaviour in Himachal Pradesh. In order to explore and understand the first question an empirical exercise is carried out in village Sungra of Kinnuar.

The exploration into what type of marriages are prevalent in the study area, as was suggested in the literature on Kinnaur, people, by and large, observe traditional marriage practices. The women interviewed for the present study irrespective of their personal or community's traditional preferences reveal that arranged marriages are quite in vogue. All of them further state that monogamy is very popular. Kinnaur being the tribal belt, clan exogamy remains an important form of marriage. One of the reasons being that the hold of family, community, traditions and the collective group sentiments continue to strongly influence the members of the Kinnaura tribe. It, however, does not mean complete presence of monolithic marriages. The socio-cultural change is also taking place in Kinnaur and in the way of life of the people of Kinnaur. This is observable from the emerging urbanism, modernisation, commercialisation of agriculture and horticulture, spread of non-formal and formal education and occupational diversification. The impact of these forces is evident from the changing preferences which some people have for the non-traditional or the popularly called love marriages.

Table 4.1

Preference for Marriage Practices

Marriage Preference	*Frequency*	*Percentage*
Traditionally practised monogamous marriage	313	79.8
Love marriages or marriage by one's own choice	79	20.2
Total	392	100.0

Table 4.1 reveals that 79 per cent of the respondents have an inclination for arranged marriage, 20.2 per cent show their preference for love marriage. The changing preferences and their acceptability among good number of women indicate some change taking place in the institutional practices. There is emergence of new value patterns. The love marriage as a concept and practice is based on the idea of western liberalism and individualism. In the west, it is believed that any person who is an adult and assumed to be a responsible citizen should be allowed to select his partner. Such type of marriages tend to begin with dating of the prospective couple for some time. Then it turns into romantic love, which, in fact, is a central cultural value. The society approves such kind of selections and accepts such marriages as normal.

Table 4.2

Acceptability of Love Marriages among the Kinnauras

Response	*Frequency*	*Percentage*
Not applicable	313	79.8
Acceptable in the community	79	20.2
Total	392	100.0

Whether love marriages are acceptable among the Kinnauras, the responses, particularly of those preferring love marriages (Table 4.2) indicate in affirmative. In the initial stages there is some resistance either from girl's parents or from boy's parents. The situation normalises in due course of time with the intervention of relatives and friends. It is interesting to note that the so-called non-traditional or love marriages have been there among the Kinnauras in the past too. The mode and manner of their solemnisation was different. Historically, a marriage called *haar* was in practice. In this a boy either kidnapped a girl or a girl eloped with her boy-friend. While the former refers to an act which makes use of force, in the case of the latter it was a voluntary decision. However, in this type of marriage the status distinctions based on social class was very important. While such marriages were considered illegal by the people of upper classes, the lower classes accepted these as a matter of pride. However, when such a marriage took place, the community in order to keep its unity and integrity accorded sanctity to it by imposing sanctions on the boy. In this process, the kinsmen mediated to settle the matter. What was initially called an offense was converted into a sacred affair with the intervention of kinsmen and the parents. The fine paid by a boy became *izat* (honour or respect) and was considered some kind of atonement for the act of kidnapping (Singh, 1988: 18-49).

Do people practise what they prefer? The data presented in Table 4.3 reveal that 79.8 per cent of the respondents had an arranged marriage. In contrast to which only 19.9 per cent went in for non-traditional or what they described as love marriage. It is understandable that those who practiced latter type of marriage also expressed their preference. They also informed that they themselves made the selection of the spouse and the proposal was carried through their relations and friends. Interestingly,

Table 4.3

Marriage Preference and the Type of Marriage of the Respondents

Marriage Preference/ Marriage Solemnised	*Arranged Marriage*	*Love Marriage*	*No Response*	*Total*
Love marriages acceptable	-	78 (19.6)	1 (0.3)	79 (20.2)
Traditional marriages preferred	313 (79.8)	-	-	313 (79.8)
Total	313 (79.8)	78 (19.6)	1 (0.3)	392 (100.0)

Figures in parentheses indicate percentages.

in the Indian society, as the examples exist in the epics, even if the marriages were arranged, the women had the liberty to accord approval to the would be spouse or make a choice from the probables presented to her by the parents. However, the choice of a male was governed by certain conditions which were to be fulfilled by one of the probables invited by the parents. This was the institution of *swaymbara*. It was a practice among the royal families. Whether this was common and all sections of the society practiced it, is very difficult to say. There is also no evidence to suggest that the practice of a *swayambra* ever prevailed in Kinnaur.

It is also found that every society has some form of traditions and practices which are not meant for formation of marital relationships but do provide an opportunity to boys and girls to meet. There are socially organised fairs and festivals or even a marriage in the neighborhood facilitating meetings of young boys and girls. At times, though very rare, such meetings result into formation of permanent relationships. It may, however, be noted that the fair and festivals are not consciously organised for the purposes of formation of marital relationships. If such a relationship develops, it is also not an intended consequence of fairs and festivals.

Table 4.4

Respondents Consent in the Selection of the Spouse

Choice	*Frequency*	*Percentage*
Not applicable	79	20.1
No response	2	0.5
Self	149	38.0
Parents	160	40.8
Total	392	100.0

Do the women having arranged marriage have any liberty in making a choice of the mate? The data presented in Table 4.4 indicate that 38 per cent of the respondents enjoyed liberty in making the choice of their would be partner. Of the total respondents who had arranged marriage (313), they constituted 47.60 per cent. The 40.81 per cent respondents in whose case the entire decision was made by the parents constitute 51.11 per cent of those who had arranged marriage. In general, there is some degree of freedom which the women enjoy in the selection of mate. This is despite the patriarchal system in Kinnaur. This change is the result of women education.

Marriage in Kinnaur, whether a case of *haar* or an arranged marriage, is a social and family affair as well. It has already been mentioned that the members of the family, kins group and the community as a whole participate. Therefore, the date and the time of solemnisation of marriage is decided by the family and relations keeping in view the *mahurat.* Unlike the Hindus, this *mahurat* is performed in the presence of the *devta* (deity) of the community. The priest who performs the rituals on behalf of *devta* decides by dedicating the action to the *devta.* On being asked majority of the respondents interviewed stated that it is both the parents who decide about the marriage. There are 49 per cent of the respondents in whose case the decision was taken by the parents. Another 30.4 per cent of them reported that the decision was taken up by their respective fathers alone. The categorisation of the responses in terms of who actually decides and what matters in such decisions, the data reveal two things. First indicates women's participation in the decision-making about their own individual life partner. The second suggests prevalence of patriarchal system in which males (father, uncle, brother, etc.) dominate. Another 20.2 per cent of the respondents who had love marriage informed that the decision regarding solemnisation of their marriage was taken first by the respondents themselves and then marriage could take place on the said date and time through the intervention of their near relatives including uncles, friends and others.

Table 4.5

Decision about the Solemnisation of Respondents' Marriage

Decision taken	*Frequency*	*Percentage*
Self with help of relatives	79	20.2
Father	119	30.4
Mother	1	0.3
Brother	1	0.3
Both parents together	192	49.0
Total	392	100.0

According to the Hindu texts and scriptures, the prescribed age at marriage for the girls is the age at which they attain puberty. Traditionally, in some communities, a marriage used to be solemnised even much earlier than the attainment of puberty, i.e., in the infancy itself. Although it is illegal under the contemporary law, this practice continues even today in some areas in Rajasthan. Under such marriages, the girl continues to live with her parents till she matures and attains puberty. However, with the changing conditions of life, education of the girls and demands of the society, the age at marriage has increased to a considerable extent, except for some areas. It is also observed that even people's conception about what should be the ideal age at marriage has also changed to some extent in the urban areas. The impact of mass-media, education, women employment and other forces of modernisation seem to have been quite vital as agents of change.

Table 4.6
Respondents' Age at Marriage

Age (in years)	*Men*	*Women*
18 - 20	206 (52.5)	382 (97.6)
21 - 22	186 (47.4)	10 (2.6)
Total	392 (100.0)	392 (100.0)

Figures in parentheses indicate percentages.

The empirical findings indicate that the maximum age which these women describe as the ideal age at marriage ranges between 18 years and 24 years and above. The former is the age propagated by the government. Table 4.6 also indicates that a maximum number of the women (52.5%) favour minimum age of marriage for men between 18 and 20 years. On the other hand, for women, 97.6 per cent of the respondents suggest 15 to 18 years as the ideal age at marriage. In general, the difference in the age of boys and girls for the purpose of marriages has also been maintained in the Hindu texts and ranges between 3 to 5 years or even more. In the case of Himachal Pradesh, it is found that on an average males marry 4.6 years later than girls (NFHS, 1992: 47). Generally, a boy is expected to be of more age in comparison to a girl. But, the opinions differ among people. In comparison to the first, there are 47.4 per cent respondents who feel that a boy should be matured enough at the time of marriage to carry on the responsibilities of the family. He should be in a position to guide his own family of procreation and orientation. Therefore, these women think that a boy must be of higher age in comparison to a girl. The minimum age described by them is 21 to 22 years. In the case of girls, only 26 per cent favour higher age and that too between 18 and 20 years. The upper limit of ideal age at marriage suggested by women is approximately the same as it is found in the case of Himachal Pradesh as a whole. The mean age at marriage in 1992 was 20.4 years. This has risen from 15.6 years in 1961 (NFHS, 1992: 47).

Table 4.7

Actual Age at which the Respondents Got Married

Actual age at Marriage	*Frequency*	*Percentage*
15 - 20	250	63.8
21 - 25	126	32.1
26 plus	16	4.1
Total	392	100.0

The empirical investigation into this aspect of women in Kinnaur revealed that 63.8 per cent of them were married between the age of 15 and 20 years, 32 per cent tied the nuptial knot between the age of 21 years and 25 years and only 4 per cent got married at the age of 26 years or more. A comparative view of the data presented in Tables 4.6 and 4.7 indicates that as far as the lower limit of age at marriage is concerned there is a gap of three years between the ideal age at marriage and the actual age at which they get married.

It is understandable that the sexual exposure particularly in the case of women in a traditional society like India, in the normative context is possible only after they are married. The incidence of pre-marital relations, is very limited. Since sexual union before marriage is socially prohibited and women are expected to be chaste, virgin, etc., they are restrained from entering into such acts. Even if such a relationship exists, it is not disclosed for various reasons including the fear of being branded as immoral. The socio-cultural expectations from women also make them observe abstinence as well as not to make public any such matter. Even if some women under certain circumstances enter into such a union secretly, they do not disclose it before others. It is precisely due to these reasons that in Kinnaur all women stated that first exposure to sex was only after the solemnisation of their marriage. It is also worthwhile to mention that in Himachal Pradesh, the rural-urban differences in the age at first cohabitation are quite visible. It is found that maximum number of urban and rural women had their first cohabitation at the age of 25 years. But it is also noted that in some cases the minimum age of first cohabitation in Himachal Pradesh has been found 13 years. However, the number of women having cohabitation at this age is minimal (NFHS, 1992: 53). In comparison to the sample of the present study, the age at first cohabitation is higher in Himachal Pradesh as a whole. In a comparative perspective this, therefore, implies that the age at first cohabitation is quite low in the tribal areas of Himachal Pradesh.

Table 4.8

Age at First and the Last Conception

Age (in years)	*Up to 25 (percentage)*	*26-30 (percentage)*	*31 plus (percentage)*	*Total (percentage)*
20 years	121 (30.8)	68 (17.3)	27 (6.8)	216 (55.3)
21-25 years	93 (23.7)	35 (8.92)	7 (1.7)	135 (34.5)
26 plus	23 (5.8)	15 (3.8)	3 (.8)	41 (10.2)
Total	237 (60.5)	118 (30.0)	37 (9.5)	392 (100.0)

Figures in parentheses indicate percentages.

In Indian society at large and in the tribal society in particular, the birth of a child is generally expected during the first year of marriage. The rationale behind this expectation is the value attached with marriage in the Hindu texts, i.e., the function of marriage is begetting progeny for the continuation of the *vansha* (the clan or the *kula*). It is also a proof of woman's normality with regard to capacity to bear children. These are significant factors in the acceptability of a married woman in the community. This also follows that the age at marriage, exposure to coitus and conception are related with each other. The data presented in Table 4.8 indicate that 55.3 per cent of the respondents had their first conception when they were of less than 20 years of age. On the other hand, 34.5 per cent of the respondents informed that they conceived the first child between 21 and 25 years of age. The remaining stated that they conceived for the first time at the age of 26 and after. The analysis of age at which the respondents had last conception Table 4.8 indicates that the last child conceived by maximum of them (60.6%) was at the age of 25 years. The number of those whose last conception fell between 26 and 30 years of age is represented by 30 per cent respondents. Only 9.5 per cent had their last conception after the age of 31 years. The data suggest that with the advancement in age, the fertility among the Kinnaura women declines. This is evident from emerging pattern of increasing age at marriage and the decreasing number of conceptions. However, it is difficult to argue whether the last conception recorded actually means last as many of them, from reproductive health point of view can still bear the children. The understanding of this fact also requires further probing into various aspects of marital life, particularly in the context of family planning practices and the number of children they have, the coitus behaviour of the couples and the period for which they have been exposed to coitus, etc.

The fertility is a biological phenomenon which depends upon the socially accepted and established union between male and female. Marriage in India is the act through which the society accords social legitimacy to man and woman to enter into coitus relation. The information on this aspect is generally not forthcoming as women feel shy even when they are talking to a woman, especially the one not known to them. However, whatever information after considerable persuasion could be ascertained from the respondents has been enumerated in Table 4.9.

Table 4.9
Frequency of Coitus

Coitus (per week)	*Frequency*	*Percentage*
Once	108	27.5
Twice	184	46.9
Thrice	97	24.7
Four times	3	.8
Total	392	100.0

The data on coitus behaviour of the couples reveal that a

maximum number of the respondents (46.9%) have coitus twice a week and one-fourth carry out this act thrice a week. There are only 0.8 per cent respondents who informed that they perform this act even four times a week. The number of those who have minimum frequency of coitus is just 27.5 per cent. This may be mentioned here that this phenomenon is related with age to a considerable extent. The frequency of coitus decreases with the increase in the age of the respondents. Although difficult to say but there is something called male menopause which may be affecting the frequency of coitus. The other factors accounting for less frequency of coitus are religious factors requiring individuals to observe abstinence during the fasting days or other occasions. At times, husband's nature of employment also makes abstinence possible.

The respondents further reveal that in almost all the cases the frequency of coitus also depends upon the sexuality of the spouse. In general, it is the male who takes initiative first for the performance of sexual activity. One of the reasons given by women for their inactivity as well as passive role is that they get tired after carrying out the household chores, agriculture related activities and looking after the family. Only one respondent told that it is she who at times takes initiative. As a matter of fact the biological needs of man and woman are the same. But the women are socialised and values inculcated in their personality make them suppress even their basic needs.

Is sex the main function of marriage? In Hindu society marriage, by and large, is considered a sacred phenomenon. One of the reasons being that in Hindu way of life, theoretically, one complete part of life is devoted to *kama*, which acts as a source of pleasure and progeny. In the case of the latter, birth of a son in the family is the most desired thing. This desire is rational-ised through the theory of *moksha*. *Putra prapti* is essential as it is the son who is expected to fulfill all the paternal obligations by way of performing last rites and post-death rites. Does the Kinnaura society also practice sex preferences as part of their religious way of life?

Table 4.10
Desired Number of Sons

Desired Number of Sons	*Frequency*	*Percentage*
0	125	31.9
1	267	68.2
Total	392	100.0

Table 4.10 reveals that as many as 31.9 per cent of the respondents categorically stated that it is immaterial to have the birth of a son or a daughter in the family. Kinnauras are a patriarchal society for all practical purposes. The no preference for son sounds strange. The probing into this issue revealed that there were no religious compulsions clearly expressed by the respondents. However, 68.2 per cent of the respondents were of the opinion that minimum one son should be there in the family. Since the girls go off after marriage, the son remains the only hope for the ageing parents. It is therefore for the reason of social security in the old age that people prefer to have a son.

Though only 31.9 per cent of the respondents did not show any preference for a particular sex but the data on desired number of daughters confirm some change taking place in the attitude of people. When asked about the number of daughters desired in a family, except for one respondent the remaining stated having a daughter is a must. This can clearly be observed

Table 4.11

Desired Number of Daughters in the Family

Desired Number of Daughters	*Frequency*	*Percentage*
0	1	0.3
1	317	80.9
. 2	74	18.9
Total	392	100.0

from Table 4.11. An overwhelming number of respondents (80.9%) prefer to have minimum one daughter and less than one-fifth (18.9%) have preference for two daughters. The reasons cited for preference for a daughter are the increasing mobility among sons to other areas, sons not taking care of the ageing parents, etc. In some cases, family was considered quite significant in bringing about change in sex preferences. The daughters are stated to be more caring than the boys in the recent times. It is also observed that in metropolitan cities parents do not find it problematic to live with any of their daughters even after the daughters are married. They even take financial help from the daughters.

Table 4.12

Desired Number of Children and Ideal Size of the Family

Family Size	*Number of Children*			
	Two	*Three*	*Four*	*Total*
Four members	158 (40.4)	-	-	158 (40.4)
Five members	-	184 (46.9)	-	184 (46.9)
Six members	-	-	50 (12.7)	50 (12.7)
Total	158 (40.4)	184 (46.9)	50 (12.7)	392 (100.0)

Figures in parentheses indicate percentages.

How many children normally a family should have? Is there a norm governing the number of desired children among the Kinnauras?---were the questions put to the respondents. The respondents suggested the range of children between two and four as can be seen from Table 4.12. In terms of ideal family size, 40.4 per cent respondents favour having two children and 46.9 per cent prefer three children. Beyond three children, the number of respondents is just 12.7 per cent.

The general trend in Himachal Pradesh is two to three children. It is, however, argued that there is also a tendency among some women to adjust their ideal family size upwards over time as their number of children increases by way of rationalisation (NFHS, 1992:118). This suggests that there is a gap between what the respondents think ideal and the number of children they have in actual. In order to examine this, data on ideal size of family conceived by the respondents and the actual number of children the couples have been analysed here.

Having discussed about sex preferences and the ideal size of the family, an attempt is made here to examine whether there exists a gap between the ideal number of children and the number of actually living children of the respondents. The data presented in Table 4.13 indicate that the total number of respondents' alive children is two and three represented by 31.9 and 30.9 per cent respectively. Those having four or more children are minimum in number. When compared with the age of the respondents, it was found that the couples who were in relatively higher age and belonged to scheduled caste families (data not presented in table format) have more children in comparison to the high castes. By and large, the families are restricted to one to three children at the most. The data also indicate that there is a difference between what is considered ideal and what in actual exists. This difference is both ways. First,

Table 4.13

Ideal Number of Children and the Actual Number of Children in the Family

Ideal Number	Actual Number					
	One	*Two*	*Three*	*Four*	*Five+*	*Total*
Two	59	73	23	3	-	158 (40.4)
Three	13	39	93	38	1	184 (46.9)
Four	5	13	5	12	15	50 (12.7)
Total	77 (19.0)	125 (31.8)	121 (30.8)	53 (13.5)	16 (4.0)	392 (100.0)

Figures in parentheses indicate percentages.

some of the respondents have less number of children than the ideal number. The reason perhaps being that they are yet to complete their individual family and desire to have an additional child. Second, those having more children than the ideal number indicate the difference between what is being propagated by the family welfare department and the actual number which the individual family has and desires. Such a difference is also due to the fact that the couples elder in age were late adopters of family welfare measures than the younger age groups. This is not only the case with the scheduled tribe areas but similarly differences have also been observed in the case of non-tribal areas of Himachal Pradesh (see Sharma, 1995). The data, therefore, suggest the possible influence of social and cultural factors, the values attached with children and other considerations on the child bearing practices.

Knowledge and Practice of Family Planning

The previous section dealt with marriage and child bearing practices prevalent among the Kinnaura women. In this section, an attempt is made to explore the existing knowledge and practice of family planning in Kinnaur. In 1992, the survey of family health in Himachal Pradesh noted 'nearly universal knowledge'. All the married women in urban areas and 99 per cent in rural areas reported knowledge of at least one method of family planning. Further, the rural-urban differences indicated 96 per cent of ever married women in urban areas and 79 per cent in rural areas spontaneously mentioned modern contraceptive methods (NFHS, 1992: 79). The rural areas show less knowledge about modern methods than the urban areas. It is, therefore, expected that women belonging to the tribal areas, like the ones in rural areas in the state are also likely to have less knowledge.

In the absence of modern family planning methods and other technical interventions regulating birth controls, the fertility behaviour in the study area was affected by the use of traditional devices. The most popular among these was coitus regulation, particularly with regard to its timing, frequency, voluntary and involuntary abstinence. Both the types of abstinence have been reported by the Kinnauras. The former refers to no coitus relation during certain period prohibited by religion. It was voluntary in the sense that people refrained from it. The latter makes a case for those conditions which compel the couples to be separate for some time. Here one can refer to the situations in which the husband goes out to some other place for employment or business. These controls might have been in some way responsible in delaying the possible conceptions.

In Hinduism, as per the traditional mode of organisation of life was concerned, human sexuality was controlled by the goals which an individual was supposed to strive for to attain four things, namely, *dharma, artha, kama* and *moksha*. Accordingly, the life was divided into four *ashrams* (parts), viz., *Brahmacharya, Grahastha, Vanprastha* and *Sanyasa*. The control over sexuality was realised by intensive religious practices even during the *Grahastha* period. This was done by avoiding certain types of food which were supposed to be exciting. Along with this there was culturally prescribed sexual abstinence during early and later part of life and also during the inauspicious occasions.

A glance into religious texts also reveals that the night was divided into four *pahars* (parts) and each *pahar* had its own significance with regard to sexual activity. In Buddhism, one finds particular timings for begetting a particular quality of the progeny. So much so that Buddhist text also provides descriptions of the positions in which a male and female need to have during the sexual act for getting a boy or a girl. In the similar manner, Hindu way of life theoretically regulated sex and thereby seems to have curbed fertility among certain sections of the society. Not going into the details of the traditional literature, it is a fact that even religious practices, if followed in its letter and spirit, acted as mechanisms of fertility control.

In India, the first formal fertility regulation policy was adopted in 1952. This policy laid down emphasis on the provision of clinical services to the people for advocating family planning. This was called clinical approach. The basic and the underlying assumption was that opening of family planning services through clinics would attract couples desirous of regulating the birth of their would be children; their fertility and limiting the size of the family. One of the fallacies committed by the government perhaps was over expectation with regard to voluntary opting for family planning by the people. Not only this, the expectation even was that the people will be coming to the clinics themselves, adopt whatever was prescribed to them by the health worker or the doctor. This policy, however, could not operate successfully over the years. The hindrance was not the lack of information to the people about the programme but the social, cultural and ritual values attached with children were found to be acting contrary to the new fertility norms preached by the government agencies and its agents, mainly the state health departments and their workers.

It was in view of the failure of the above mentioned policy that after almost one decade the government had to think of alternate strategies. Instead of asking people to visit clinics, the reformulated alternate policy framework laid down emphasis on the extension of family planning services to the people. The underlying assumption was that by offering services to women at their doorsteps, more and more families would come under the purview of the programme. The trained family planning workers, auxiliary nurse midwives (ANMs), medical and paramedical staff was assigned the role of motivators. They were expected to visit married women in their homes and motivate them for regulating their child bearing practices and thereby restrict the size of their families. The extension approach also incorporated mother and child health programme in the policy. With the addition of the said, the family planning programme was made a multipurpose health programme. One of the problems with this programme, however, was that in terms of coverage it remained quite limited. Therefore, the government was compelled to formulate a more focused family planning scheme. A number of small programmes were undertaken. One of the approaches adopted in this process of rethinking was known as "Maxi Camp Approach" (Sharma, 1994).

Under this programme, family planning camps were organised and sterilisation was conducted on the people. One of the characteristics of these programmes was achieving the targets fixed by the state. This was also called "target approach". It is important to note that these camps were organised at various places without caring for the scientific, hygienic conduciveness of the place where the sterilisation operations were conducted. The compulsion for the medical and the paramedical staff was realising the targets fixed by the government. Therefore, a large number of people were brought to these camps for meeting the targets fixed by the overenthusiastic political leadership. Some of the sterilisation operations were unsuccessful and resulted in various adverse complications---physical as well as psychological. The lack of follow-up services further complicated these cases. Ultimately, the programmes as a whole, in some states, resulted in less success and more problems.

Reflecting on the entire approach to family planning in India, Bose (1988) observed that when the family planning programmes were started for the first time, there was almost a complete absence of expertise in demography in India. Therefore, the early programmes remained mere experimentation rather than a holistic policy. He further remarked that the Planning Commission which started with this kind of exercise also committed blunders. It assumed the population growth rate of 1.25 per cent per annum on the basis of previous census conducted during the decade 1941-51. It was a blunder because the population growth rate was already rising and it had recorded 2.2 per cent between 1951-61.

Mehta (1998) refers to the predicaments in the whole planning exercise in terms of equating demographic profile with family planning programme by the Government of India. There is no doubt that there was great enthusiasm and the family planning programme was launched with a vigorous note.

Consequently, there was a rapid growth of such services and centres. From just 147 family planning clinics in the year 1956, the number of primary health centers (PHCs)----a higher level of health facility, reached 5,500 in 1980. The number of family welfare centres and sub-centres in 1980 increased to 5,400 and 15,500 respectively in the rural areas. However, the massive growth fell short of the desired. Taking a critical look at the initiation of the programme, Mehta (1997) dubbed this programme as a "Rocket". The reason being that most of these health centres remained understaffed, dumping grounds for expired medicine stocks, out-dated equipment and one may also add that even the doctors posted in these far off and remote areas were not for making the services efficient and accessible to people. The doctors stayed there for the posting tenure without much interest for the service of the community. Once their tenure was over, they left the areas not to return back. In fact, the widespread feeling which prevailed was that a posting to rural and remote area was a kind of punishment.

The implication of the aforementioned facts of the medical services in general and family planning programmes in particular was that these services in the tribal and rural areas were virtually defunct or non-functional. The health centres were staffed by qualified (those who hold professional degree) but apathetic doctors. The function which these doctors and other paramedical officials performed most efficiently was issuing of certificates to the people which stated that sterilisation operation has been performed on them. On the basis of the same, these doctors presented inflated figures of achievements. This was done consciously. To a considerable extent, the officials committed such irregularities in order to please the political bosses.

Premi (1998) draws our attention towards the population

policy which came into being in 1976. The new policy emphasised on the population control with special reference to its two-fold objectives and role envisaged in it. First, its significance in the movement towards economic independence, and second, bringing about social transformation of the society with particular reference to the then highly propagated and ongoing 20-point programme of the Government of India. Following this policy, the state governments also introduced certain incentives and disbursement of cash rewards to those undergoing sterilisation operations. This was done to encourage the general population to adopt family planning. The state and the central government employees in particular were given additional increments as incentives to go in for sterilisation operations. This had some impact as some employees did undergo sterilisation operations in order to earn additional increments.

At this juncture, it may be noted that the period between 1976 and 1979 was very crucial from the point of view of family planning programmes. The use of coercive methods was also made in the implementation of family planning programme, particularly during the period Sanjay Gandhi enjoyed unlimited political power and influence in decision-making in the centre. It is a matter of some consideration from two angles. First, did the coercive method only increase the numbers or it qualitatively helped in the implementation of the programme? Second, is such a policy tenable in a democratic setup?

The use of force in carrying out sterilisation was anti-democratic and therefore, it became a political issue in the post-emergency period. It was politicised by the then newly formed Janata Dal which later came to power. The government softened its stand, reversed the policy and put emphasis on the voluntary family planning. In this way, the policy remained indecisive and the Planning Commission, Government of India appointed a working group on population policy in 1979. The group suggested long-term measures. One of the goals was to achieve Net Reproduction Rate (NRR) of one by 1996. The other goals emphasised reductions in the family size, birth rate, death rate and infant mortality rate. The other indirect measures included raising the age at marriage, elementary education to all the girls of school going age and improvement in the child nutrition through policies like midday meals.

Premi (1998) further refers to the issue of integrating the population and family welfare programme with the MCH programme including universal immunisation literacy programmes. He argues that the problem with the programme has been that the education department of the concerned states did not make much headway in this regard. The basic purpose of universal female education as emphasised in the draft of the policy was that it would have definite impact on fertility behaviour in two ways. First, by way of raising the age at marriage, it would delay child birth. Second, education would induce change in the attitudes towards smaller family size by enlightening people. It is believed that a programme can be a success only when the people are motivated. These ideas have been mere ideals and desires which received a mixed response as far as their impact was concerned. A critical appraisal of the policies reveals that in the implementation of the programmes considerable emphasis was put on the role of government officials and agencies. Unfortunately, nowhere the programme attempts at involving the people at the grassroots level. Therefore, whatever was done, by and large, remained official programmes with very little inputs from the community by way of participation. In this way, most of the issues forming part of family planning programme and policies, even today, remain far away from those population groups whose general fertility levels are quite high. Such programmes could provide better results if the people at the grassroots level were involved as participants in the execution of the programmes.

Himachal Pradesh has been following the policies and programmes of the Government of India for the implementation of the family planning. The state has a network of sub-centres, primary health centres, community health centres, postpartum centres, and various voluntary organisations to carry on the family welfare programmes at the district, tehsil, block and panchayat level. In comparison to other states the population growth and density in the state has been low. In the 1991 census, while Himachal pradesh had 20.79 per cent population growth India as a whole registered 23.85 per cent. Even in terms of sex-ratio, literacy rate, couple protection rates, life expectancy, etc. Himachal Pradesh indicates higher standards in comparison to rest of the country. This is also an indication of possible use of contraception---both the traditional methods and the modern ones. The family welfare programme is voluntary, leaving the choice of the method to the individual couple. It is also noted that in the implementation of the programmes there is a good use of mass media and interpersonal communications and this helps in removing the socio-cultural barriers (NFHS, 1992: 9).

In Kinnaur, the knowledge of different methods of family planning varies between 44 per cent for injections and 99.8 per cent for pills. Kinnaur which constitutes one of the notified scheduled tribe area has been quite successful in the implementation of modern contraception. The data released by the state health department with regard to achievements in implementing the family planning methods in the recent times is quite revealing and quite encouraging.

The data with regard to sterilisation indicate that in 1990-91, Kinnaur had almost 75 per cent achievement. This increased to 101.4 per cent in 1991-92 and 101.6 per cent in 1992-93. However, in 1993-94 the achievement level fell to 83.20 per cent. This downward trend in achievement could be the result of earlier high achievement levels. Even though reduced, the trend remains quite appreciable provided it does not fall further. The other area in which considerable progress has been achieved is the couple protection rate. The data for Kinnaur indicate that in 1983 about 29.1 per cent eligible couples were brought under the protection cover and the number reached 47.99 per cent in 1996. The achievement with regard to other devices, such as IUD (Intra Uterine Devices), use of condoms, oral pills and utilisation of other family welfare services indicate considerable differentiation. The trends, however, in the use of condoms, oral pills and family welfare programmes show upward progress, especially during 1990-91 to 1992. Somehow, after that the percentage achievement have been on the decline. Keeping in view the trends prevalent in Kinnaur district, a question arises as to what are the factors underlying the use of contraception, particularly in relation to women.

In the absence of an empirical study, it is difficult to argue with regard to the reasons or factors for the use of contraception. However, some tentative explanation can be given on the basis of secondary sources. Mhloyi (1996: 61) argues that status of women is important in fertility determination. What makes the difference is the nature and type of socio-cultural milieu in which the women are placed---the lineage system, patriarchy or matriarchy. In the context of status of women and family planning, these premises are stated to be somewhat defused or widespread: First, the psycho-social satisfaction. This is determined by the respective socio-economic contexts of the person concerned. Second, children as survival strategy or an insurance against life chance risks. Third, family planning used as a means to achieve the articulated desired family size. Besides, the factors constituting as indices of status of women are education, labour force participation, occupation and income (Mhloyi, 1996: 63).

To begin with the empirical analysis of knowledge of respondents with regard to family planning methods in Kinnaur is made at two levels. First, the description of their knowledge and practices. At the second level, the status determinants of family planning practices, if any are analysed. The first question related to the knowledge respondents have about family planning methods. They were initially reluctant and shy to name the methods. However, with some prompting by involving them in discussion about family planning methods they named a few. Except for two respondents, the others stated some methods indicating thereby that they have knowledge of various devices which are available to the people for the planning of their individual family.

Table 4.14

Methods Named by the Respondents

Methods	*Frequency*	*Percentage*
No/not applicable	2	.6
Pills	3	.8
Condom	49	12.5
Copper-T	97	24.7
Sterilisation	241	61.6
Total	392	100.0

According to data presented in Table 4.14 the maximum number of the respondents (61.6%) are aware of sterilisation operation method. The other 24.7 per cent mentioned the use of IUD for avoiding conceptions. The use of methods like condom popularly known as *Nirodh* is mentioned by 12.5 per cent, and *Mala-D* pills by a very few respondents. All these methods are the ones widely advertised through the mass-media or the electronic media by the state. Most of these women learnt about these methods from other women. What is important to note here is that the permanent method, i.e., sterilisation, is very popular. This is also due to the fact that in Kinnaur this is a very popular method as indicated by the achievements of family welfare programme published by the state health department from time to time.

It is well known that both the central and state governments have carried out massive propaganda about family welfare measures. The emphasis of which have been on the diffusion of knowledge of family planning methods among the masses in general. To accomplish the goals of family planning various agencies and trained manpower has been involved. It has been shown in Table 4.14 that these measures have been popular among the people of Kinnaur, though the impact has been differential. A visit to the area of fieldwork, however, reveals that the diffusion of knowledge in the hard conditions of life is not an easy task. The knowledge which people have is suggestive of the fact of effective implementation of the programme with the help of different sources, agencies and the manpower.

The data presented in Table 4.15 with regard to sources of knowledge of family planning methods indicate that 17 per cent of the respondents did not state any source and learnt about these methods in the course of their married life. However, in the case of 28.1 and 21.9 per cent the source of information was health workers and the mass-media, mainly television, radio

Table 4.15
Source of Knowledge of Family Planning Method

Source of Knowledge	*Frequency*	*Percentage*
Not applicable	2	0.6
No source	67	17.0
Doctor	41	10.5
Health worker	86	21.9
Husband	42	10.7
Friends	44	11.2
Media	110	28.1
Total	392	100.0

and newspaper, respectively. The others acquired information from the qualified doctors (10.5%), their respective husband (10.7%) and friends (11.2%). The data, therefore, suggest that in the study area a large number of agencies---both formal and informal---have been acting as the family planning agents. The role of media and health workers in particular seems to have been very effective. In this regard, it may be further argued that the effectivity of health workers and media rests with their capacity to reach the people and the kind of somewhat informal relationship which they are able to establish with the people at their doorsteps.

The knowledge about a method is available to the people through various sources in the contemporary Kinnaura society. Whether the knowledge acquired by them is put to practice was another question asked from the respondents. This was done in order to probe into the issue of practicing of family planning devices. The idea was whether they also have knowledge about using the various family planning devices available to them. The query revealed that except for three respondents all of them replied in affirmative by stating that they knew how to use these methods. The other question asked pertained to what method respondents themselves have been using in avoiding unwanted pregnancies. The discussion held with them revealed that they do not use any one particular method. They have been using more than one method. The maximum number of the respondents reveal that they have been using condom and spacing technique in an alternative manner. The reason given by them was that these methods are easy to practice. The condom is also easily available. Although some risk is always involved in the use of both the methods, but these, as per their experience have been quite safe. Those who talked about these methods numbered 36.7 per cent of the total. The other method used quite popularly is IUD by 26.5 per cent respondents. The use of pills and condoms alone has been made by 6.6 and 10.2 per cent of the respondents respectively. Besides the said, one person has under gone sterilisation operation after using pills and Copper-T for some time. In addition to it, there are 26.5 per cent others who have adopted permanent method by undergoing sterilisation operation. The data therefore indicates that the respondents are not only aware of various methods but have also been using them in planning their family. The data presented in Table 4.16 also conform to the official records with regard to the use of various devices available to the respondents. However, a comparative analysis of data in Table 4.14 and 4.16 indicates no relationship between their knowledge of method and the actual method used by them. Why does variation exist in the method named as known and the method actually used by the women? One of the reasons perhaps is the initial inhibitions women have with regard to revealing their knowledge of family planning methods which are considered as personal. The other reason is that the use of methods is not generally decided by the women.

Table 4.16

Methods Used by the Respondents

Methods	*Frequency*	*Percentage*
No method	71	18.1
Pills	26	6.6
Condom	40	10.2
Copper-T	4	1.0
Operation	104	26.5
Spacing	147	37.5
Total	392	100.0

The issue as to who takes decision with regard to the use of family planning methods was discussed with the respondents. It was found that in the case of 62.8 per cent of the respondents the decision was taken by the husbands as is evident from the data presented in Table 4.17. On the other hand, only 18.9 per cent of the respondents reported that the decision was taken by them.

Table 4.17

Decision for the Use of Methods

Decision Maker	*Frequency*	*Percentage*
Not applicable	72	18.4
Husband	246	62.8
Self	74	18.9
Total	392	100.0

This is an expected phenomenon that in matters in which the reference to female body comes, the women are generally either not forthcoming or they are not permitted to take decisions. In the case of those women who stated that they themselves took the initiative in this regard, some of them revealed that they are compelled by the burden of pregnancies and children which they have to carry. In order to keep their health good they made their men use some method or they threatened them that they would themselves resort to the use of some method. The women feel that since they have to work at home and in agriculture, they cannot afford to bear more children. Such a bold step is indeed unique in the socio-cultural context of Indian society in general and the Kinnauras in particular. Nevertheless, it is the most important development which is taking place in Kinnaur.

One of the common observations regarding the acceptance of any technology is that in the initial stages its use is often resisted by the people. In the case of practising family planning methods there have also been certain socio-cultural impediments which, at times also restrict the use. Such a tendency is found among those groups who consider child birth as a gift of god or treat it more as a natural phenomena. The process of acceptance and practising of a technology, therefore, requires some motivation either at the level of the individual him/herself or through some external agencies.

From sociological point of view, the motivation is not inherent within the individual but the source lies in the external world surrounding the human beings. The data presented in Table 4.18 indicate that there are different sources of motivation enumerated by the respondents. The source-wise percentage distribution of response indicates that the motivation came minimum from doctors (6.1%), in good number from health workers (19.9%) and friends (17.9%). It is interesting to note that 35.8 per cent women state that they were motivated by

Table 4.18
Sources of Motivation

Source	*Frequency*	*Percentage*
Not applicable	2	.5
Selt	74	19.0
Doctor	24	6.1
Health worker	78	19.9
Husband	140	35.8
Friends	70	17.9
Media	4	1.2
Total	392	100.0

their husbands. These women are those who had gone for sterilisation operation. Why have the women undergone tubectomy? It is a belief among the men that if they undergo vasectomy they lose their *takat* (vitality). That is the reason why the husbands motivate their wives for sterilisation. Further probing in this respect revealed that the respondents' husbands convinced them with some logic by making suggestions. What motivation meant here was that the women were induced to go in for permanent contraception by their husbands. The health worker is found as another most effective agent in the spread of contraceptive information through personal contacts with the individuals and the community. The role of health workers is very significant in the entire process of implementation of family planning programme.

The data presented in Table 4.19 indicate reason-based favourableness about the practice of family planning. Among them, 27.8 per cent stated that the practice of these methods is good as it prevents unwanted births. Another 28.1 per cent argue that one of the factors responsible for women's ill health is

Table 4.19
Respondents' Views about the Use of Contraception

Views	*Frequency*	*Percentage*
No response	71	18.0
Birth control	109	27.8
Good for women health	110	28.1
Useful in preventing STDs	102	26.0
Total	392	100.0

uncontrolled and frequent pregnancies, abortions, miscarriages, etc. Prevention of more births helps the women in maintaining good health. Another 26 per cent of the respondents referred to prevalence of various diseases, especially the sexually transmitted diseases (STDs) in the contemporary times. It is common place observation that electronic media, particularly television, gives lot of coverage to most of the sexually transmitted diseases. Even posters and other visuals are put up in the village health centres (sub-centres, PHCs, etc.). These silent mediums, if not effective, minimum inform people about the possible diseases which one can contract.

These women think that many of these diseases can be prevented with the use of family planning devices particularly with the use of condom. On being asked about the diseases, the women, however, failed to respond. The data, therefore, indicate that at some level of their conscious or subconscious mind they also have a fear of catching a disease. This fear, as it appears, possibly also acts as a contraceptive itself.

At times, for the purposes of minimising the size of the family, some people prefer to go for induced abortions. The abortion is a legal way of termination of pregnancy. But its practice is generally not favoured in public on account of two reasons. One, it amounts to killing of the foetus, and therefore, a sin against god. Second, going for abortion is misunderstood as it among some groups implies something wrong with the health of the women. Therefore, a community may not approve such a practice. Among the Kinnaura women, abortion, by and large, is not practised. The data presented in Table 4.20 indicate that only 8.9 and 2 per cent respondents had one and two induced abortions respectively. This implies that in majority cases, the women do not terminate the pregnancy voluntarily.

Table 4.20

Number of Induced Abortions

Abortions	*Frequency*	*Percentage*
Nil	349	89.0
1	35	8.9
2 plus	8	2.0
Total	392	100.0

Table 4.21

Number of Miscarriages

Miscarriage	*Frequency*	*Percentage*
0	270	68.9
1	103	26.3
2	15	3.8
3 plus	4	1.1
Total	392	100.0

The incidence of miscarriages, which is not within the control of the pregnant women and can happen due to certain accidental factors, seems to be quite high among the Kinnauras. The data presented in Table 4.21 reveal that 26.3 per cent of the respondents had miscarriages. The number of such cases is certainly very high. It is possible that some of the respondents described induced abortions as miscarriages due to certain cultural factors. However, further probing suggests that working in the agricultural fields, doing heavy work and other hazards of life of the Kinnaura women could be the other possible reasons leading to such a problem during the period of pregnancy. Another reason cited by a couple of women holds men responsible for this mishap. The problem arises due to lack of precautions in coitus during the pregnancy. In some cases (3.8% and 1.1%) the number of miscarriages have been two and three respectively. The data, therefore, suggest that reproductive health of women in Kinnaur seems to have some problems and therefore, needs a detailed study.

The foregoing discussion with regard to marriage, child bearing and family planning practices is quite revealing. It is found that in the contemporary times people, by and large, tend to go in for monogamous marriages in accordance with the culture and traditions of the Kinnaura society. There is not even a single case who reported of having polyandry in the family. In the monogamous marriages both arranged and love marriages are practised. The latter may not be a new phenomenon as the Kinnauras practised a marriage called *haar* which was either through kidnapping of the girl by a boy or a girl eloping with her boy friend. The role of kinsmen was very important in facilitating such marriages. This was functional as it helped the family or the group to maintain its unity.

In the case of arranged marriages, the women do enjoy some liberty in giving approval for the mate chosen initially by their parents. This is confirmed by the empirical finding that in the choice of the mate a good number of women's consent was taken by their parents. The society being patriarchal, the hold of males continues to be quite strong in the matters concerning solemnisation of marriages, etc. The marriage practices have another important component, i.e., age at marriage. With regard to the ideal age at marriage the women suggest 18 years for girls and 21 years for boys which is also propagated through the media. However, in practice more girls get married at the age less than the age of 18 years. In comparison to girls, more boys are found getting married at a later age, i.e., after the age of 21 years.

The Kinnaura women, contrary to the general impression that it is a promiscuous society, do not practice premarital sex. Accordingly, respondents' exposure to coitus and the first conception is related with their age at marriage.

The child bearing, as per the general expectation, the women should bear the child in the first year of marriage. This expectation is a social binding and there are number of rituals associated with it. The sex preferences among the Kinnauras reveal that the respondents desire to have minimum one son. This desire is based on the Hindu texts according to which it is the son who should perform the last rites. But contrary to the belief that girls are not preferred, the data provide sufficient evidence in which people also think of having minimum one girl child in the family. Some even indicated their desire to have two daughters. There is no socially set ideal number of children in Kinnaur. The number of desired children varies from family to family. The ideal size of the family and ideal number of children are associated with each other. Those who want to have two children suggest four member family as the ideal. With an addition in the number of children, a corresponding addition also takes place in the size of the family. The ideal number of children is four and the members of the family is put at six. However, like the ideal age at marriage, there is significant difference in the number of actual children of the respondents and the ideal number. At the same time, it is also found that there are respondents whose actual number of children is less than the ideal number told by them. In their case, their age is less and the family is not complete. This is, therefore, evident that the marriage and child bearing practices among the Kinnauras are not monolithic. There are variations which may have been caused by the structural differences between the respondents. The relationship between the number of children a family has and the status of women will be discussed at length in the sixth chapter.

The general response to the family welfare programmes in Himachal Pradesh seems to have been quite encouraging. The data from secondary sources on the use of family planning devices in Kinnaur district reveals that the permanent methods are quite popular. This is particularly the case with reference to the people undergoing sterilisation operations. The empirical data also point out that except for one case, all the respondents have knowledge about one or the other method of family planning.

The knowledge about these methods is acquired by them from various sources, namely, the health worker, doctor, husband, friends and media. Among these sources the role of media and the health worker is reported to be more popular. There are about one-fifth of the respondents who say that they did not have any source of knowledge. It may, however, be mentioned that knowledge comes from external sources. Therefore, in these cases they may have got some information from some source but they are unable to mention.

With regard to the use of different methods by the respondents themselves, the data revealed that both the traditional as well as modern methods of family planning are in vogue. A good number of them use spacing and as many as little more than one-fourth of the respondents have undergone sterilisation operation. These methods are most popularly used. The decision with regard to the use of different methods is made by the husbands. The health worker is an important source for the respondents' use of family planning devices. One of the reasons is that lot of educational work is carried out by the health department workers. There are non-governmental organisations too which act as educators. The women seem to be conscious about their health and therefore, they think that the use of contraception is good for them and the family. It is also substantiated by the fact that people in the study area remain in touch with health professionals.

5 Structural Correlates of Reproduction

In the previous chapters, an attempt was made to explore and describe various aspects of social structure, status of women, nature of women's work participation and their role in decision-making in the family, prevalent marriage, child bearing and the family planning practices in Kinnaur. It was obvious that besides being a society governed by the values of patriarchy, the social structure of Kinnaur is characterised by the socio-cultural and the economic factors. In the changing times, some of the variables such as caste, education, income, occupation, etc., seem to play an important role in the overall life of the people. As a matter of fact, these variables, not only describe the set patterns of relationships but also account for variations in the relative social status of people in general. Social status, which represents the sum total of one's or one's group's social standing in relation to others is of great significance in the determination of life chances and lifestyles of the people. In the context of fertility behaviour, social status is considered to be quite critical. The prevalent assumption is that higher the status of women (socio-economic as well as cultural), the lower is the number of children ever born to them (United Nations, 1996: 32).

It is important to note that the conventional status attributes in the study of fertility behaviour included, family income or husband's income, educational status of the head of the household, husband's occupation, number of family members economically dependent and independent, the property held by the family, caste status, and so on (Mahadevan, 1979: 87). In the contemporary times, the society has witnessed a change in the status of women, particularly in the case of those who have moved into employment outside the home and are living in the urban areas. Such women represent middle class, work in the organised sector and enjoy relatively more economic and social security. There is another, but a larger group of women working in the unorganised sector, which remains low-paid or under-paid, do not enjoy any privilege. In this way, employment, sector of employment and nature and type of employment have also become important indicators of women's status in the society.

The other variables identified by the Ford Foundation (1991) have already been mentioned in the section dealing with methodology. To mention once again for the purpose of analysis, these include: education, nutritional status, dignity in the society, i.e., the social recognition of women, access to food, access to medical care, length of pregnancy intervals, number of children born including still-births, premature abortions, number of survivals, maternal mortality, control over sexuality, early or late exposure, participation in decision-making process, cultural values such as age at marriage, social norms governing life of women, income, occupational status, right to spacing and number of children, etc. Although these variables are very important, but the understanding and analysis of these become difficult due to socio-cultural inhibitions prevalent among women.

Since the present study deals with a rural setting notified as the scheduled tribe area, there are many other local factors and conditions which need to be taken into consideration. The women in Kinnaur, as witnessed in the discussion on socio-economic profile, mostly work in the unorganised sector and most of them perform labour on their family farms. In such a situation, gender disparities in terms of the amount of work women do everyday and recognition that work gets them in terms of economic gains are very significant in determining their status (Devi Lalitha, 1982). It may be noted that the gender disparities are constructed on the basis of patriarchy and other socio-religious themes which have been important elements in the social organisation of Hindu society. The existence of disparities in Kinnuar are based on the distribution of family resources between men and women. Being a patriarchal system, the control over movable and immovable properties always remains in the hands of the male members of the family. In this way, social and cultural factors further limit the women. There are religious rituals which put women in a position of subordination. This has reference to the reverence which an Indian woman is expected to have for her husband. The concept of *patiparmeshwar* makes her accept the domination of male. The interplay of social, religious and economic factors makes the line of distinction between a male and a female very rigid.

Historically, being in a subordinate position for all practical purposes, most of the women ever since their childhood are socialised in such a way that they have household orientation more than any other thing. Therefore, most of these women remain confined to the four walls of the house. The carrying out of the household chores by the women is based on the basic sex based division of the society. But their household work is not attached with any economic value. This amounts to denial of justice to women. What is considered significant is the generation of additional household income. Paradoxically, it has also been observed that even when a woman does paid work outside home, her working outside is looked at in an ambivalent manner. Such an attitude, perhaps also has a negative impact on the psychology of women.

At this juncture, it is also important to argue that the women, as is obvious from the foregoing discussion, do not constitute a homogeneous category. Therefore, the various factors which may sound as having a limiting impact, do not influence women in a uniform manner. The impact is differential as the status enjoyed by women tend to be differential. In other words, the status of women varies in accordance with their class and caste, the educational level, the nature and type of occupation followed by them. The education and work are the two variables which have been internationally recognised as important, particularly in the context of fertility (United Nations, 1985). The other factors are the religion and the ethnicity which are stated as having considerable influence on fertility. In the case of the Kinnauras, the ethnic question, however, cannot be taken as in their case it is same for all. It is also observed that both religion and ethnicity only act as subjective measures of high or low status for the individual or the group. But they are not taken as objective criteria of status determination in the democratic set-up.

In some of the studies on fertility, education, economic participation, health status, legal status of women are considered as important. The relationship worked out in statistical terms reveals significant association between these variables and fertility (Kazi and Sathar, 1986). However, among the said factors, Easterline (1984) described education as crucial. But, the impact of education is not always direct. It is visible only through different channels. Easterline has identified three ways. First, the impact of education depends upon the supply of children a couple can afford to have. In the second case, fertility depends upon the demand for children which a couple desires with particular motives underlying this demand. It means the basic reasons for having a desired number of children. The third refers to the difficulties which a couple may face in the regulation of fertility. Under this factor, there are many things involved, namely, money, time cost, knowledge about methods of family planning, the access to those methods and the attitudes which the people have towards having children matters in a significant manner (Easterline and Crimmins, 1982). Similarly, the impact of education on the supply of children especially when the absence of contraception is felt in four ways. It is stated that education delays entering into marriage alliance. Also, the duration and intensity of breast-feeding comes down with the increase in the education of women (Sharma et al., 1990).

The cultural factors imposing abstinence and taboos are also likely to decline among educated women (Oni, 1985). It is observed that when the contraception is absent all the said factors affect birth intervals. In the case of better educated women, these are likely to be shorter than those who are less educated. The fourth way refers to the relationship between education, infant and child mortality. The educated women take care of health of the child in a much more better manner than the less educated women. This is likely to cut down the demand for more children.

There have also been studies indicating somewhat weak association between education and fertility, even in the case of developed countries (Hubback, 1975; Mahadevan, 1979: 33). The inverse relationship, it is believed, rests on peculiarity of circumstances during the demographic transition phase. With the change in these circumstances the relationship may acquire a different nature (Kiser, 1971; Mahadevan, 1979: 33). The educational status of women in the developing countries is very different from those of the developed countries. Although literacy rates in India have gone up phenomenally in many states, but the dilemma persists whether these are mere statistical manipulations or actual literacy. In view of which the argument that in developing countries inverse relationship between education and fertility may not have universal confirmation holds true to a greater extent.

In the context of fertility, particularly with reference to the Theory of Demographic Transition, the development level of a society may be stated as affecting the status of women. In this regard, it may be noted that Himachal Pradesh in India is among those few states having highest literacy rate and it is also more developed on the social scale. The female child literacy is high. The official records maintain that 90 per cent of the school-age girls are attending schools. The number of school-going girls at present cannot be taken as helpful in bringing down the birth rates. Whether it is going to have a positive impact in the future is difficult to say as there are also certain impediments in women education. It is observed that enrollment of girls in schools does not ensure continuity in schooling and guards against drop-outs in future. At present, the fact remains that less than half of women in the child-bearing age are illiterate. The status of women as per the official reporting is low. The women are discriminated in many spheres, the consequence of which is the lower female literacy, lower child immunisation rates, higher female child mortality rate, severe malnutrition, etc., (NFHS, 1995).

The above mentioned are some of the significant trends observed in the context of relationship between status variables affecting the fertility behaviour. In the context of present study, this chapter tends to analyse the relationship between women status and fertility by taking into consideration the following variables: caste, education, income, occupation, work participation in labour force, decision-making, age at marriage, marriage practices, voluntary abstinence, knowledge and practice of family planning, etc.

To begin with caste, a social structural category determined by the structured social and economic inequalities and "perpetuated through various socio-cultural themes" (Mahar, 1972), is considered important from the point of view of determination of fertility behaviour. It has also been noted that in the social structure of Kinnaur, caste acts as a crucial factor of status distinctions.

Table 5.1

Caste and the Number of Children Born

Caste	*Number of Children Born*					
	1	*2*	*3*	*4*	*5+*	*Total*
High castes	55 (20.75)	98 (36.98)	84 (31.69)	20 (7.54)	8 (3.01)	265 (100.00)
Scheduled castes	22 (17.32)	27 (21.25)	37 (29.13)	33 (25.98)	8 (6.29)	127 (100.00)
Total	77 (19.64)	125 (31.88)	121 (30.86)	53 (13.52)	16 (4.08)	392 (100.00)

Figures in parentheses indicate percentages. Chi-square = 31.20092 significant at .01 level, d.f. = (5-1) (2-1) 4.

The data presented in Table 5.1 on caste-wise distribution of number of births given by each of the respondents reveal an inverse trend. Among the high caste, the maximum number of the respondents have given birth to one to three children. The fertility differentials within the high caste show that number of women with one child is only 20.75 per cent. Most couples, as discussed in the previous chapter, wish to have minimum two children. Therefore, the number of women with two children is 36.98 per cent. However, the number of women with three children declines to 31.54 per cent. The decline is gradual as many couples in their mid 40s have three children. This has been an acceptable norm in the mid-60s. However, with the increase in the number of children from three to four and five-plus the number of women registers a sharp decline to 7.54 and 3.01 per cent respectively. This trend indicates that among the high caste, the prevailing tendency is to have two to three children. A very small number prefer to go in for more than three children. In comparison to them, the data in the case of scheduled castes indicate that majority of the respondents have a tendency to go in for more than three children. The internal variations indicate that till the number of children reaches three, the number of respondents indicates gradual increase. However, the number of respondents with four children show a declining trend. But this decline is quite moderate, i.e., from 29.13 per cent to 25.98 per cent only. In comparison to those having only two children, the number of respondents with four children is relatively higher. This is also in sharp contrast to the high castes, particularly in the case of those who have four or more children. The chi-square value of 31.20092 (significant at .01 level) indicates highly significant differences between the fertility trends present among the high and the low castes. The statistical analysis, therefore, indicate that the scheduled castes among the Kinnauras tend to have larger families in comparison to the high castes, mainly the Rajputs. Although there are some respondents among the high castes who also have four or five children, but the number of such cases is quite small.

Table 5.2
Respondents' Education and Number of Children Born

Education	*Number of Children*					
	1	*2*	*3*	*4*	*5+*	*Total*
Illiterate	0 (0.0)	21 (27.27)	18 (23.37)	28 (49.35)	10 (12.98)	77 (100.00)
Primary	7 (11.66)	17 (28.33)	20 (33.33)	13 (21.66)	3 (5.00)	60 (100.00)
Middle	35 (29.66)	42 (35.59)	35 (29.66)	3 (5.00)	3 (5.00)	118 (100.00)
Matric	29 (23.57)	40 (32.52)	45 (36.58)	9 (7.31)	0 (0.0)	123 (100.00)
B.A.	6 (46.15)	4 (30.76)	3 (23.07)	0 (0.0)	0 (0.0)	13 (100.00)
M.A.	0 (0.0)	1 (100.00)	0 (0.0)	0 (0.0)	0 (0.0)	1 (100.00)
Total	77 (19.64)	125 (31.88)	121 (30.86)	53 (13.52)	16 (4.08)	392 (100.00)

Figures in parentheses indicate percentages. Chi-square = 68.49135, significant at .01 level, d.f. = 16.

Education, often termed as the vehicle of change, is found to be significantly related with fertility behaviour. The nature of relationship is generally inverse. This implies that higher the education, lower the fertility and vice versa. In the light of the prevalent observation and which has also been proved across the cultures and held as true, the analysis of association between education and fertility have also been carried out in the context of the Kinnaura women.

The data presented in Table 5.2, with particular reference to the above referred to observation, is quite revealing. It is found that the respondents in the illiterate category, in larger numbers, tend to have more children. In terms of education, there are considerable differences between those who have one to three children and those who have four and five children. It is found that with the increase in the level of education, i.e., up to primary school level, the picture of fertility changes with more concentration in the one to three children category. In comparison to respondents in illiterate category, in primary school category of education a sharp decline is visible in the number of those who have four and five children respectively. A somewhat similar trend is also observed in the case of middle school educated respondents. In fact, it is observed that the number of respondents having four and five children respectively is much lower in the successive higher education category than the respondents in the lower education category. There is, however, a little fluctuation in the case of the respondents having high school education. Among these respondents, the trend seems to be having three children. Even in the case of four children category there is slight increase in the number of respondents. A cross examination of the data with caste indicate that a good number of these respondents come from scheduled castes category. This, therefore, also acts as an indication of the fact that education alone does not matter. There are various other factors which may also be influencing the fertility behaviour among certain sections of the population. However, in the next higher educational categories, i.e., graduation and post-graduation, the concentration increases in the one and two children category. When the number of children goes beyond two, the data indicate considerable decline. The analysis, therefore, reveals that leaving aside the exceptions, by and large, there exists an inverse relationship between education and fertility even in the tribal districts. It may be mentioned that Kinnaur is sufficiently developed as far as various health facilities are concerned. Therefore, education coupled with other developmental attributes of the individual and the group affect the fertility among the Kinnaura women. The statistical measurement of the education-wise fertility differentials is found to be highly significant (Chi-square 68.49135 significant at .01 level).

Having examined the association between respondents' education and fertility, an analysis of the husbands' education and the fertility are also important, especially when we see that in a patriarchal society, the women's status is subservient to that of the status of men, and they have little say in the affairs of the household, even including the matters pertaining to the number of children a family thinks of having, etc. This, therefore, also raises a question: Do women have a choice to go in for a child or not to go? In relation to respondents' education, it is possible that their husbands' education may be more pervasive. The underlying assumption here being that, at times, husband's education and his, relatively higher social status than his wife may be more effective in determining fertility differentials.

The data presented in Table 5.3 indicate much in line with the expectation. The respondents' husbands with no education have three to five children with more concentration in the four and five children category. Those who have primary to middle education indicate a shift of concentration from four to five children to maximum concentration in the one to two children category. The maximum number, however, is concentrated in the two children category. In comparison to women's education, their husbands' education seems to be more influencing. It is quite surprising to note that in contrast to the primary and middle category, the number of children is higher among those who have matriculation qualifications. It is notable that in the one child to three child category, the number of respondents' husband is increasing. The increase, however, declines after second child. But the number starts falling further down with the

Table 5.3
Husbands' Education and the Number of Children Born

Education	*Number of Children Born*					
	1	*2*	*3*	*4*	*5+*	*Total*
Illiterate	-	-	5 (23.80)	8 (38.09)	8 (38.09)	21 (100.00)
Primary-middle	34 (33.33)	49 (48.03)	16 (15.68)	3 (2.94)	-	102 (100.00)
Matric	30 (15.46)	54 (27.83)	60 (30.92)	42 (21.64)	8 (4.12)	194 (100.00)
B.A.	13 (19.69)	18 (27.27)	35 (53.03)	-	-	66 (100.00)
M.A.	-	4 (44.44)	5 (55.55)			9 (100.00)
Total	77 (19.64)	125 (31.88)	121 (30.86)	53 (13.52)	16 (4.08)	392 (100.00)

Figures in parentheses indicate percentages. Chi-square = 156.3929, significant at .01 level, d.f. = 12.

increase in the number of children. The similar trends are also visible in the graduation and post graduation categories in which the number of those having one child is 19.69 per cent, two children 27.27 per cent and three children 53.03 per cent. Another surprising finding observable in the present context is that those who have post graduation in percentage terms are concentrated in the two and three children category. It may be argued here that this kind of result is more due to a very small number of respondents falling in the higher education category. A larger sample may help in getting the expected results. The statistical measure also indicates an unusually higher level of significance. Although such fertility differentials are ought to be there when an association is established between husbands' education and the levels of fertility. It is also possible that there are other factors such as income of the household and occupational status which may be intervening more effectively in enhancing the level of significance.

Table 5.4

Respondents' Occupation and Number of Children Born

Occupation	*Number of Children Born*					
	1	*2*	*3*	*4*	*5+*	*Total*
Housewife	-	-	2 (22.22)	5 (55.55)	2 (22.22)	9 (100.00)
Housewife and agriculture	76 (20.15)	120 (31.83)	119 (31.56)	48 (12.73)	14 (3.71)	377 (100.00)
Government service	1 (16.66)	5 (83.33)	-	-	-	6 (100.00)
Total	77 (19.64)	125 (31.88)	121 (30.86)	53 (13.52)	16 (4.08)	392 (100.00)

Figures in parentheses indicate percentages. Chi-square = 32.1984, significant at .01 level, d.f. = 8.

Although the data presented in Table 5.4 on women's occupation do not show much diversification, but the three major occupational categories do reflect on the inverse trend between occupation and fertility among the Kinnaura women. The occupational division indicates that those who are simply housewives and do not work outside the homes have children ranging between three to five. In relation to them, the women who work as housewives and in agriculture have maximum number of children in the one to three children category. There are some who have four and five children but the number of such women is very small. There are only six women who work in the government offices. They have only one to two children. On the basis of this, it is difficult to make any conclusions. However, it may be stated that if larger sample with more diversification in occupations is taken for analysis, the trends may be very clear. However, the hypothesis that the women who work outside their home have lesser number of children than those who remain at home seems to be quite valid. The statistical score of chi-square (32.1984 significant at .01 level) confirms occupational classification affecting fertility differentials.

Table 5.5

Husbands' Occupation and Number of Children Born

Occupation	*Number of Children Born*					
	1	*2*	*3*	*4*	*5+*	*Total*
Government service	35 (25.17)	48 (34.53)	49 (35.25)	7 (5.03)	-	139 (100.00)
Business	11 (20.00)	31 (56.36)	13 (23.63)	-	-	55 (100.00)
Agriculture	31 (16.48)	46 (24.46)	59 (31.38)	44 (23.40)	8 (4.25)	188 (100.00)
Artisan	-	-	-	2 (33.33)	4 (66.66)	6 (100.00)
Construction worker	-	-	-	-	4 (100.00)	4 (100.00)
Total	77 (19.64)	125 (31.88)	121 (30.86)	53 (13.52)	16 (4.08)	392 (100.00)

Figures in parentheses indicate percentages. Chi-square = 110.4142, significant at .01 level, d.f. = 16.

Like the education of the respondents' husbands, the analysis of their occupation and number of their children is also analysed in order to see if there is any influence of husbands' occupation on fertility (Table 5.5). Such analysis also become significant in view of the argument that under patriarchal system, it is the men who decide all matters pertaining to the family. The occupational classification and the number of children the family has indicates that those in the government service have children between one and three. The concentration is more in the two and three children category. The similar trend is visible among those who are carrying on some kind of trade and commercial activities at their village level. In this category, maximum number have two children. One possible reason which can be cited here is that those who are in such occupations do not remain confined to their home. They, at time, go outside their village for certain business activities due to which they observe some kind of abstinence and therefore, the chances of conception are reduced accordingly. There may be other reasons too. May be, being in business, they also make cost-benefit analysis while considering having of an additional child.

In the other agricultural category, the distribution of number of children indicates that maximum number (31.38%) have three children. The number of respondents' husbands indicates upward movement up to three children. However, the number starts falling with the increase in the number of children to four. It substantially declines when the number of children rises to five. One of the reasons often cited is that the agricultural families go in for more children because of their family farm labour needs. But the trends indicate that after three children there is general tendency not to have any additional child. The data also reflect on the highly significant statistical association (chi-square 110.4142 significant at .01 level) between the occupational categories and the number of children. This, therefore, implies that in the given social and cultural setting the fertility differentials are to a great extent caused by the occupational differences. A comparative analysis of respondents' occupation and the occupation of their husbands, from the statistical point of view the occupation of the husband seems to be more effective than the occupation of women. This may also be mentioned here that the occupational differences between the respondents, however, have been very little in comparison to the occupational differences between their husbands.

The income of respondents' household, as observed earlier, seems to have an inverse relationship with fertility behaviour due to two reasons. First, based on the idea of demographic transition theory, it is argued that higher the income of the household, lower is the level of fertility. The rationale behind this argument is that with more income the affordability of the family to maintain a good health increases and the chances of child mortality decrease in the family accordingly. This, therefore, results in lesser number of children born in a family. The other associated argument with this is that when a household has higher income, both the child and the mother have better level of nutrition. The other reason which is contrary to the above is based on the studies of fertility behaviour in the neighbouring states of Punjab and Haryana conducted during mid-1980s. It suggests that when the economy is in transition, there is a emerging consciousness for social mobility even among the poor families. Therefore, they with lower income would like to have lower number of children so that their children are able to have upward social mobility. How far this argument is tenable in the case of the Kinnaura women in Himachal Pradesh is examined here.

The data presented in Table 5.6 on the household income and the number of children born indicate that among the respondents placed in the lowest income group, i.e., less than Rs. 1,000 a month, the majority of them have three to four children. In comparison to them a very small percentage has one to

Table 5.6

Household Income and Number of Children Born

Income (in Rs.)	*Number of Children Born*					
	1	*2*	*3*	*4*	*5+*	*Total*
Up to 1,000	2	5	20	20	5	52
	(3.84)	(9.61)	(38.46)	(38.46)	(9.61)	(100.00)
1,001-2,000	28	51	55	22	4	160
	(17.5)	(31.87)	(34.37)	(13.75)	(2.5)	(100.00)
2,001-3,000	23	41	40	11	7	122
	(18.85)	(33.60)	(32.78)	(9.01)	(5.73)	(100.00)
3,001-4,000	5	7	6	-	-	18
	(27.77)	(38.88)	(33.33)			(100.00)
4,001-5,000+	19	21	-	-	-	40
	(47.5)	(52.5)				(100.00)
Total	77	125	121	53	16	392
	(19.64)	(31.88)	(30.86)	(13.52)	(4.08)	(100.00)

Figures in parentheses indicate percentages. Chi-square = 84.01258, significant at .01 level, d.f. = 16.

two children. With the rise in income to Rs. 1,001 to Rs. 2,000 per month the fertility behaviour indicates a change. In this category, relatively smaller number has four and five children. The majority of the respondent have one to three children. What is common between the two categories is the maximum of the respondents falling in the three children category. However, with further rise in income to Rs. 2,001 to Rs. 3,000 per month, the trend acquires a new shape. First, the number of respondents is gradually increasing in the one child category. Second, the number of respondents in the two children category goes up slightly in comparison to the first two categories. The data further show that even in the higher income categories the number of those having one to two children is increasing in comparison to those who, have three to five children. What is significant to note is that there is no one in the higher income categories having more than three children. The data, therefore, confirms the view that income differentials are sufficiently reflected in the fertility differences. The statistical enumeration of the income and fertility differences reveal a highly significant inverse relationship between the differences of the two. It, therefore, also implies an association between income and fertility differentials.

Table 5.7

Type of Marriage and Number of Children Born

Marriage Type	*Number of Children Born*					
	1	*2*	*3*	*4*	*5+*	*Total*
No response	-	-	1 (100.00)	-	-	1 (100.00)
Arranged	42 (13.41)	92 (29.39)	107 (34.18)	53 (16.93)	16 (5.11)	313 (100.00)
Love/ courtship	35 (44.87)	30 (38.46)	13 (16.66)	-	-	78 (100.00)
Total	77 (19.64)	125 (31.88)	121 (30.86)	53 (13.52)	16 (4.08)	392 (100.00)

Figures in parentheses indicate percentages. Chi-square = 56.48453, significant at .01 level, d.f. = 4, calculated on the basis of 391 cases.

Besides the directly status determining variables, there are a number of intervening variables which also have a direct bearing on the fertility behaviour. One such may be the type of marriage. In the chapter on marriage and child bearing practices it was stated that not many studies have been conducted on the relationship between type of marriage and fertility behaviour.

However, it was contended that there may be some relationship between the two. In order to understand whether there exists a relationship or not an attempt has been made here to find out the existing trends. The data presented in Table 5.7 indicate that those who have arranged marriages, the number of children born to them ranges between one to five. A large number of them had two and three children. It is interesting to further note that all of the respondents who have four and five children had arranged marriages. On the other hand, those respondents whose marriages took place through their personal arrangements and were mediated through relationships for social acceptance have relatively lesser number of children. First, there is no one who has more than three children. The other interesting demographic feature about them is that a maximum number among them have one child and then two children. The number of those having three children is very small. Why this type of trend is there? This question requires further analysis of these respondents in terms of their social and economic status. The factor responsible for lesser number of children is that most of these respondents are of relatively younger age group. Secondly, unlike those who had arranged marriages, these respondents had to manage their home themselves. What it, therefore, implies is that it is not the love marriage as such which is responsible for the small size of their families. But it is their existential conditions which prevented child birth. In addition to these two reasons the third was the relatively better education of these respondents. The application of chi-square as a measure of association between the marriage and fertility differences discerns a highly significant relationship. This further implies that within a given population the type of marriage does has its impact on the child-bearing practices of the people.

Table 5.8

Age at Marriage and Number of Children Born

Age (in years)	*Number of Children Born*					
	1	*2*	*3*	*4*	*5+*	*Total*
15-20	54 (21.60)	67 (26.80)	74 (29.6)	43 (17.20)	12 (4.80)	250 (100.00)
21-25	21 (16.66)	56 (44.44)	36 (28.57)	9 (7.14)	4 (3.17)	126 (100.00)
26+	2 (12.5)	2 (12.5)	11 (68.75)	1 (06.25)	-	16 (100.00)
Total	77 (19.64)	125 (31.88)	121 (30.86)	53 (13.52)	16 (4.08)	392 (100.00)

Figures in parentheses indicate percentages. Chi-square = 27.54346, significant at .01 level, d.f. = 8.

The other factor associated with type of marriage is age at marriage. It has been influencing the fertility behaviour in a significant manner. It is, therefore, contended that those who get married at an early age have a relatively longer reproductive span and therefore, the probability of higher fertility levels also increases significantly. The data presented in Table 5.8 in this regard indicate that those respondents who were married between the age of 15 to 20 years have one to five children. The maximum number, however, is placed in the one to three children category. The discernible trend is that in this category the number of children increases from one to three. It reaches the maximum number of three and then indicates a decline. In comparison to this category, the respondents who got married at a later age, i.e., between 21 to 25 years of age, the maximum number of children born to 44.44 per cent respondents is two. In this category, the number of children increases from one to two in a significant way. But the number of respondents declines to

28.57 per cent in the case of those who have three children. After three children the number of respondents comes down significantly. The similar trend is also discernible in the case of those respondents who were married at the age of 26+ years. However, in this category the maximum number of children born to 68.75 per cent is three. This is contrary to what has been witnessed in the previous age at marriage group. It is also noted that in this category those who have one and two children their percentage is too little. But this trend may not be a pattern as the number of the respondents in this age at marriage category is too little. A bigger sample may provide a continuous pattern of fertility among the Kinnauras. At this juncture, it is worth arguing that as per the expectation, the data in the context of age at marriage and fertility behaviour do provide an evidence of inverse relationship. The differences in age at marriage and fertility are again highly significant with chi-square showing 56.48453 at .01 level of significance.

Table 5.9

Duration of Continuous Sexual Exposure and Number of Children Born

Duration (in years)	*Number of Children*					
	1	*2*	*3*	*4*	*5+*	*Total*
1-5	52 (60.46)	34 (39.53)	-	-	-	86 (100.00)
6-10	29 (24.16)	41 (34.16)	50 (41.66)	-	-	120 (100.00)
11-15	-	25 (36.23)	27 (39.13)	17 (24.63)	-	69 (100.00)
16-20 and plus	-	25 (21.36)	44 (37.60)	32 (27.35)	16 (13.67)	117 (100.00)
Total	77 (19.64)	125 (31.88)	121 (30.86)	53 (13.52)	16 (4.08)	392 (100.00)

Figures in parentheses represent percentages. Chi-square = 239.634, significant at .01 level, d.f. = 12.

The fertility studies conducted in the early 1960s and 1970s demonstrated a definite relationship between duration of continuous sexual exposure and fertility. Keeping in view the theoretical assumptions of those studies this aspect was also examined in the case of the Kinnaura women. In this regard, the data presented in Table 5.9 indicate that the range of continuous exposure spans between one to five years to 16 to 20 years and plus. It is further visible that the women who have shortest span of sexual exposure have maximum of two children. The data further indicate that as the span of continuous sexual exposure is increasing the number of children is also rising. What is significant to note here is that the women who have been married for 6 to 10 years the number of children in their case has increased to one to three. Those who have 11 to 15 year span, in their case the number of children has gone up from minimum 2 to maximum of 4, and those who have 16 to 20 years continuous sexual exposure in their case the number of children has gone up to 2 to 5. The number is found to be progressively increasing with the successive increase in the span of married life and sexual exposure. It is in view of this that some communities used to enforce some kind of abstinence by way of periodic temporary separation between the couples. The most common practice used to be going of the wife to her parents' home during festival days or for the performance of certain rituals.

Like exposure to sex, the frequency of coitus is also important in the determination of the number of children a couple can have. However, this is further subject to the use of contraception by the couples during coitus. The inquiry made in this regard from the women indicates that the respondents' coitus behaviour, by and large, is normal. The data presented in Table 5.10 discern that the majority of the couples just have coitus once or twice

Table 5.10

Frequency of Coitus and Number of Children Born

Duration (in years)	*Number of Children Born*					
	1	*2*	*3*	*4*	*5+*	*Total*
Once	35 (32.40)	48 (44.44)	25 (23.14)	-	-	108 (100.00)
Twice	42 (22.82)	59 (32.06)	62 (33.69)	21 (11.41)	-	184 (100.00)
Thrice	-	18 (18.55)	34 (35.05)	32 (32.98)	13 (13.40)	97 (100.00)
Four +	-	-	-	-	3 (100.00)	3 (100.00)
Total	77 (19.64)	125 (31.88)	121 (30.86)	53 (13.52)	16 (4.08)	392 (100.00)

Figures in parentheses indicate percentages. Chi-square = 188.285, significant at .01 level, d.f. = 12.

a week. Their total number constitutes 27.55 per cent and 46.93 per cent respectively. In comparison to them, only 24.24 and 0.76 per cent respondents have coitus three and four times respectively. In terms of its relationship with the fertility behaviour the data indicate that those who perform sexual intercourse once a week the number of children in their case is restricted to one to three with maximum number having two children. The number of three children in their case is only 23.19 per cent. In comparison to these respondents those who fall in the twice a week category the number of their children varies between one to four. It is important to note that in this category, the maximum number of the respondents have three children. Similarly, in the next category of coitus the number of respondents having three children is represented by 35.05 per cent. This number is higher than those having three children in the previous category. It is further noted that here the number of children goes up to even five. The number of those having four and five children is also higher in comparison to the previous category. Although, it is difficult to argue on the authenticity of the data on coitus behaviour of the respondents, but from Table 5.10 it appears that there is a definite and inverse relationship between coitus behaviour and fertility behaviour. The statistical analysis further indicate a very highly significant trend (chi-square 188.285 significant at .01 level) of differences of fertility with regard to the differential coitus behaviour of the respondents. At this point, it is important to mention that the intervening variable preventing fertility is the use of contraception by the respondents. This is said as the use of permanent method is very high among the respondents as well as in the study area.

It is believed that the intensity of work participation may be found to be related with fertility behaviour. The basic assumption here being that the women involved in work outside the home find it unmanageable to have more children. There are many reasons which account for this. At times, the nature of employment, status of the job, chances of social and spatial mobility, etc., may also account for lesser number of children born to a woman. In the case of present study, the nature of employment of the Kinnaura women is not very complex that may involve considerable fertility differentials. However, the hours of work done by women may have a bearing on the fertility. Keeping in view this assumption, the analysis of hours of work participation at home and outside the home have been carried out see the fertility differentials.

Table 5.11

Hours of Household Work and Number of Children Born

Hours	Number of Children Born					
	1	*2*	*3*	*4*	*5+*	*Total*
Five	40 (18.51)	55 (25.46)	63 (29.16)	43 (19.90)	15 (6.94)	216 (100.00)
Six	31 (19.13)	66 (40.74)	55 (33.95)	10 (6.17)	1 (0.61)	162 (100.00)
Seven	6 (66.66)	2 (22.22)	1 (11.11)	-	-	9 (100.00)
Eight +	-	2 (40.00)	2 (40.00)	1 (20.00)	-	5 (100.00)
Total	77 (19.64)	125 (31.88)	121 (30.86)	53 (13.52)	16 (4.08)	392 (100.00)

Figures in parentheses indicate percentages. Chi-square = 44.42291, significant at .01 level, d.f. = 12.

With reference to their domestic work and fertility it is obvious from the data presented in Table 5.11 that women who state that they carry on household chores for five and six hours daily have one to five children. In the distribution of the number of children it is further discernible that among these women maximum number, however, has two and three children. The difference between the two is that while in the first category the number of three children is represented by 29.16 per cent, in the case of second category the two children is represented by 40.74 per cent of the respondents. This difference is an indication of the fact that with increase in the number of working hours, the number of children starts falling. This is further substantiated by the case of women who work for seven hours. In their case, also, the maximum number of children born to them is restricted to one, two and three, and that too showing a progressively declining trend. But this trend is disturbed somewhat by the 8 hours a day work category where the fertility is on the slightly higher level. Like some of the other variables discussed above, this unusualness may be due to small size of the respondents in this category.

Table 5.12

Hours of Other than Household Work and Number of Children Born

Hours	*Number of Children Born*					
	1	*2*	*3*	*4*	*5+*	*Total*
Three	-	15 (20.00)	42 (56.00)	10 (13.33)	8 (10.66)	75 (100.00)
Four	51 (23.72)	58 (26.97)	65 (30.23)	38 (17.67)	3 (1.39)	215 (100.00)
Five	18 (19.35)	51 (54.83)	14 (15.05)	5 (5.37)	5 (5.37)	93 (100.00)
Six plus	8 (88.88)	1 (11.11)	-	-	-	9 (100.00)
Total	77 (19.64)	125 (31.88)	121 (30.86)	53 (13.52)	16 (4.08)	392 (100.00)

Figures in parentheses indicate percentages. Chi-square = 106.7882, significant at .01 level, d.f. = 12.

The women of Kinnaur besides working in their own homes also carry on agricultural and other type of employment related activities outside their homes. This additional work certainly puts both physical and mental strain on them. Whether this type of activity is also associated with fertility is an additional issue examined here. According to the data, it is clear that the minimum number of children which the women have is two and maximum they have is five. Among the women doing additional three hours work outside, maximum of them (56%) have three children. In the next higher hours of work category the concentration of the respondents increases in the one and two children category. Consequently, the number of respondents in the three children category declines accordingly. But it increases in the four children category. An exploration into the causes of this increase is that the total hours of work (inclusive of household work) done by these women is less than the others. It is here that the association between the hours of household work and fertility is further confirmed by the data. In the five hours a day work outside the home, it is further discernible that the concentration of women with two and one child further increases in a substantial manner, particularly in the two children category. In view of the statistical analysis of the data enumerated in Tables 5.11 and 5.12, it is quite obvious that the chi-square values of 44.42291 and 106.7882 respectively indicate that work-wise differences in fertility behaviour are significant. Thus, indicating the possible inverse relationship between the work participation and the fertility behaviour of the respondents.

To summarise the foregoing analysis of data, it is quite discernible that the social and economic indicators of social status of women and various other intervening variables have a significant association with the differential fertility behaviour in the study area. In other words, it may also be argued that the social and economic factors influence fertility behaviour of women in a considerable manner in a given social and cultural setting.

6 Conclusions

The perpetuation of the organic life all over the universe is guided by the process of sexual reproduction. The plants in a natural state multiply under the influence of climatic factors and other bio-geochemical cycles. The wild animals procreate under the natural conditions, and their fertility is unregulated and accidental. The domesticated animals' reproductive behaviour is influenced by the decisions of the owner. The human beings in their primitive stage of existence procreated and considered the process of sexual reproduction as part of their natural instincts and need satisfaction. The gradual departure from the natural state made human beings think of a more regulated, systematic and stable life.

The regulatory mechanisms in a human society, beginning in the last phases of the primitive stage and to the contemporary modern life, has become part of a well-defined system of social interaction, social relationships and social institutions. The modern family, representing a set of patterned relationships and well-defined modes of interaction between members, provides an example of considerably regulated life. Thus, human society at large enjoins upon its members to participate in its various affairs in accordance with the expected standards. Sumner (1906) argued that there are popular usage and traditions which the society develops during the process of its growth. These are often conducive to societal welfare and therefore, exert a pressure on the individuals to conform to them. It is perhaps not wrong to state that these regulatory mechanisms helped the human beings depart from their natural state and lead a more structured social life. When these mechanisms were adopted in the sphere of sexual reproduction is difficult to say. The structured social life, its increasing complexities and the elementary division of labour based on sexes must have had influenced the human mind to regulate sexual reproduction. But it means that, though reproduction is a natural phenomenon and forms a part of natural needs, it has come to exist as a highly regulated behaviour within the given cultural framework of human society.

In fact, in society, it is the human beings whose own efforts make them depart from their natural state of existence by evolving somewhat common norms. The members of the society, by and large, conform to these norms and the process of institutionalisation, over a period of time, facilitates this conformity. This is not, by any means, to suggest that there is no violation of the norms, nor to say, there is any society in human history where violation has not been there. But the tendency among the average persons in any society is to fear the violation. Such persons are always worried about their personal image and feel that the violation of the norms by them may result in loss of their prestige in the society (Homans, 1950).

It is also important to mention that the norms and their operation, like the existing variations in the lifestyles of the people, may not be homogenous within and across the societies.

Merton (1957: 375) refers to 'privileged norms' which operate in a restricted way and insulate the client from ready observability of their behaviour and beliefs held by others in their given role-set. But the role of social structure in influencing human behaviour, both from non-Marxist point of view (e.g., Durkheim, Parsons, Radcliffe-Brown, Malinowski and Merton), as well as Marxist perspective, is very significant. Marx, though differs from others and talk of mode of production as the crucial determining force of the superstructure of the society, the fact, however, remains that the human behaviour is always regulated and oriented towards the system which operate at a given point of time. The superstructure of the society creates a social consciousness which sways away majority of the people in a society.

The reproductive behaviour is also institutionalised and carries the differential influences of social structure. Therefore, the constraints which a social structure exerts on different strata of people make the regulatory mechanisms operate in a heterogeneous manner. This is empirically verified by Murdock (1949:286-87). He argues that regulations vary widely in different cultures; relatives with whom intercourse and marriages are strictly forbidden in one society are often privileged or preferred mates in another. Even within the same society, taboos frequently apply to certain relatives but not to other kinsmen who are genealogically closer. The extent and magnitude of variability in the application of norms within a society increased further with enlightenment and the emerging value of individualism. In other words, the more complex is a social structure, higher is possibility of variations in the operation of regulatory mechanisms.

The situation in the human society became very complex with the advent of industrial revolution. It set in a dual process of development. On the one hand, it marked the beginning of an era of economic rationality, developments in the fields of science and technology, greater division of labour with more interdependence between the interacting units, thus, giving an impression of higher order of unity. On the other hand, it led to separatism, erosion of community structures and communitarian way of life.

With regard to use of population control mechanism, it was the publication of Malthus's essay which made people conscious of increasing dangers of growing population. It warned against the possible rise of food problems due to rapid growth of population. The implication of Malthus's essay was that it not only linked the population question with development but also initiated a debate on how to control the growing population. The modernising societies with capitalist development acted as a model of change for the third world countries. Thus, these nations not only became market conscious like the countries of the first world but also induced a consciousness regarding the size of the family, the number of children a family should have etc.

The Indian society resorted to the introduction of family planning methods immediately after attaining independence. The efforts, as discussed earlier did result in acceptance of family planning measures even in some of the remote regions and consequently decline in the fertility levels. The case of BIMARU states, however, indicated failure of the family planning programmes. The analysis of reasons of failure in the implementation of these measures are very many. What we understand is that the policy-makers while devising these programmes were guided by instrumental considerations and expected the implementation of various programmes in a mechanical manner. In the process, the efforts lose sight of the values a community attaches to the child birth. It is the gap between the efforts of the state and the values of the society which remain unbridged and therefore, consequent failure of the programmes occurs. This reminds us of what happened during the period 1975-77 in many states in India. The forced sterilisation led to strong community reactions, protests and resentments. The implication of such historical experience is that in a society characterised by wide-ranging social, cultural and economic variations any programme of sensitive nature must take account of these facts before its implementation. The family welfare programmes are sensitive as they concern with sexual behaviour and people in general do not like others to intervene.

Kinnaur, a notified scheduled tribe area, from anthropological and sociological point of view, constituted a simple society with some trade with China. The trading activities were largely confined to local non-industrial products. The trade with China, however, came to an end after 1962. The people of Kinnaur depended more on agriculture for their livelihood. The local weaving catered to the woolen cloth needs of the society. In this sort of activities, the role of women remained quite important. People's dependence on the primary sector of economy and domination of patriarchal value structure determined the place for men and women. While most of these attributes continue to characterise Kinnaur even today, some change is in offing, caused especially by commercialisation of horticulture, shift from traditional cropping to cash crops, commissioning of hydel electric power projects, and the occupational mobility among men. It is worth mentioning that like the Meenas of Rajasthan, a good number of the people of Kinnaur have made it to the state administrative services and central services. Its location being of strategic importance, the means of transportation and communication have developed at a good pace. The life of women is also undergoing change with some educational mobility and quite a few even making to certain prestigious occupations. The latter is the case with women from those families where the men have entered into positions of power and privilege. In the rural areas and that too among the peasant families the education has not made the women mobile. Although the social life in Kinnaur is increasingly departing from the traditional lifestyle and losing some of its traditional characteristics by becoming more formalised and impersonal, yet the hold of traditions continues in some form or the other.

One of the most important features of change is the emerging dualism in its social structure in which the tribal sentiments, and the caste and class distinctions exist simultaneously. The social classes as such are not visible due to the stronghold of kinship ties over the individual but these exist in, somewhat, fluid form. The process of class formation has already set in with the emergence of a strong lobby of administrators, other high-ranking officials and the political elite coming from some families. Such developments are conducive to attitudinal changes and act as a base for emerging social consciousness with ego-centric tendencies among the people at large Hollingshed and Redlich (1958: 82) referred to expression of such tendencies in the form of three types of clubs. These include the one sex club (gentlemen's and ladies' clubs), the family club and the special interest club. In brief, the new developments, wherever they take place, set in the process of substitution of universalism by particularism which ultimately leads to individualism. In the context of procreation, such tendencies possibly also result in gradual reduction from reproduction for the group life to reproduction of the family life. This is perhaps due to such thinking even the modern state makes efforts in the area of fertility regulation by concentrating on couple protection rather making a policy for the group or the community protection. The consequence of such efforts is that the respective value system of the state and the community remain at variance, thus, leading to limited success of the programmes. The further implication of such a policy, at times, is that the efforts go against the basic community norms and create problems.

However, over the years, the values related with children in a given social group have remained quite in vogue, the idea of population control has also been institutionalised. With the increasing individualism and consciousness about social mobility, the state also starts expecting that the couple-oriented efforts would yield more results at the level of the community. But the society at large being in the transition phase, the social structure with a combination of both the traditional and modern values operates as a pervasive force and thus, influences the fertility behaviour in a mixed manner.

The empirical situation with regard to social structure and fertility behaviour in Kinnaur suggests that women, central in the process of child birth, have a subordinate position in relation to men. This structurally ordained low position reflects significantly on the life of women. They not only work at home but also go to agricultural fields to supplement family income. The process of their socialisation with feminine orientation renders them relatively less educated with very little choice to be mobile in the society in relation to men. Even if some women have higher educational qualifications they are constrained by the family life. They, therefore, cannot afford to move away from home for employment. This is particularly the case where the women are married off at an early age. The implication of this fact of the life of women in Kinnaur is that a higher age at marriage may help them have mobility and consequently reduce fertility levels further down. The higher age at marriage is certainly a need in Kinnaur as most women, as per the sample get married at an early age, i.e., between the age of 15 and 20 years.

It is observed that age at marriage, besides being a cultural factor, acts as an important variable of fertility determination. In Kinnaur, it is found that women entering into marital union at relatively younger age have high fertility than the women who got married at a relatively higher age. Some of the scholars believe that women who marry at ages beyond 20 years, tend biologically to reduce births (Davis, in Mahadevan, 1979: 23). It, therefore, may not be wrong to say that with the rise in age, it is not only the reproductive span which is reduced but even their physical capacities to bear and carry a child reduce gradually. Since the purpose of marriage in India is progeny, the lower age at marriage seems to be more fulfilling the progeny need. But this remark is not to suggest a lower age at marriage, but only to point out that values attached with marriage and the values of the state to raise the age marriage remain at variance.

The lower age at marriage for women in most societies have been the direct manifestation of the patriarchal system in which the women always had a dual image and status. It was a moral obligation of the group of origin to protect the honour of their women--mother, wife and, particularly the daughter. The honour of the women was the prestige of the group. This was indeed a most difficult obligation to perform, as it also required the suppression of women. In the Arabic world, circumcision was performed on the young girls to suppress their sexual desire. The other problem was as to who will take the girl of the group as a wife if the girl had violated virginity. Therefore, the group used to be highly protective of the women. This was the reason why women under patriarchy were considered a burden.

Moreover, marrying of the girl to other group member required giving of dowry. The practice of dowry is not peculiar to the Indian system but it also prevailed in France. It is observed that in France the chances of marrying off a girl depended on her dowry, a legally protected and customarily managed affair in the interest of the family (Johnson, 1983: 164). Dowry, then was a share of the family property given to the girl at the time of the marriage. Since the system of marriage required a woman to leave the home of her parents, she was not accorded any property rights. Similar consideration might have also been there behind the denial of property rights to the Kinnaur women. This was also a way through which the family's immovable property was protected from going to the other family. This is also true of Kinnaur where a woman does not have any property rights. The implication of which is that in the home of her husband and parents-in-law the woman has to live a subdued life. The women in private do explain some of their unhappy experiences on account of their no assets. Another implication of woman having no property is the perpetuation of patriarchy over the ages. In this way, patriarchy creates material conditions within itself not only for its survival but also for its continuation.

One of the tendencies among the menfolk found in Kinnaur is putting the women on work in the home as well as in the family's agricultural or horticultural lands. Although by way of doing work at home and in the agriculture they contribute immensely to the production of social life, yet their work remains unappreciated in the world of men. Due to such constraints of the social structure, the women not only feel deprived but also find themselves having no right over even themselves. This is further substantiated by the levels of women's participation in the decision-making process of the family.

In Kinnaur, the society at large looks at men as 'the important, in all family matters. The women, in general, do not have any participation in the decision-making process of the family. If they have some say, it is largely ineffective. It is the men--father, husband, brother and other male relations, who decide all social and economic matters. Even in the case of having an additional child or not, the women who actually carry the burden are rarely consulted. The only exception seems to be the age factor which seems to have some place of respect and regard. It is observed that a daughter-in-law as a woman and in the presence of elders in the family does not have any say. However, her mother-in-law carries the decisive voice in the affairs of the family. It is perhaps an arrangement which suits the husband to maintain a balance between his relationship with his wife and parents. It may be right to say that the patriarchal system vests authority in the elders, which is functional to the family system as a whole. Therefore, a woman within the family is empowered after attaining a particular age status, and especially when there also lives a woman in subordinate position in the family. Along with age, the ownership of property or no property also plays an effective role in the decision-making process.

In the matters concerning marriage practices, the Kinnauras go in for monogamous marriages which are solemnised in accordance with the traditions of their society. This is to mention that monogamy co-existed with polyandry in this region. But the practice of polyandry seems to be on the decline as no one from the study sample reported practice of polyandry among their near relations. It may be mentioned that even in polygon societies (practicing polygamy and polyandry) monogamous unions were "considerably common due to the fact that economic conditions in most of the societies favoured it" (Murdock, 1949: 28). The growing complexities of social and economic life in the contemporary society do not allow either form of polygyny to persist. It is also noted that in Kinnaur individualism is increasingly becoming dominant. It is, therefore, instrumental in the avoidance of polyandry and encouraging monogamous marriages. It is also observed that with regard to polyandry the binding on the women to go for it, wherever it may be in practice, does not exist.

It was stated earlier that Kinnaur is not a monolithic society. The form of marriage practices is also being influenced by the general trends in the larger society. It also not being an isolated area the emerging trends acquire acceptability among the people. The marriage by one's own choice among the girls is not an exception. In fact, such marriages also have the community approval, though afterwards and conditional. The latter pertains to paying of some fine or making offer of a gift to the girl's parents by the boy. It is considered as a token of respect and regards for the elders, commonly called *izzat*. It may also be noted that the persons who matter in all these affairs are the male members of the clan who facilitate such marriages by their effective interventions.

The social structure is permissive to women only as long as it is functional and suits the interests of the Kinnaura men. One area of partial freedom is mate selection. The girl may be asked to approve a boy already selected by the parents. Although most girls would approve the boy without any hesitation. However, if a girl has certain reservations then the parents do consider them and give a serious thought to the matter. The father remains the ultimate authority as for as solemnisation of marriage and other related matters are concerned.

The general impression about the tribal societies, historically, has been that these are promiscuous and permissive. Murdock (1949) noted that out of 250 societies which he studied only 34 societies permitted the men to have premarital relations and that too within the prescribed limits. For example, with brother's wife, wife' sister etc. The notable fact about this is that it was the man who had the privilege. No woman on her own could go in for such a relationship. The data about Kinnaur suggests that premarital relations do not exist as a permissive phenomenon. However, in the changing time with increasing opportunity for boys and girls to meet at places away from home, such relationships cannot be ruled out. Even in the societies where the strictest rules were imposed (about 50 years ago), the rules were broken sometimes (Kinsey, 1953). The situation is much changed now and the possibility of premarital relations becoming popular among women cannot be completely ruled out. In the light of field data, the time when the women of Kinnaur have an exposure to sex and enter into coitus relationship is the time of their marriage. In most cases, the women also conceive at this time. The implication of this is that the age of the couple is an important factor in the initiation of fertility process.

The child-bearing practices are associated with marriage and the general expectation among the Kinnauras is that a woman should bear a child within the first year of her marriage. This is considered functional as it proves the capability of both men and the woman to produce a child. In case a woman gives birth to a son, her acceptability increases considerably in the community. This is substantiated by the fact that most families prefer to have minimum one son. This is a value preferred in Hinduism. According to this, a son is must for the performance of the last rites. In case a son is not there to carry on the ritual obligations, according to the belief system, the dead person does not get salvation. However, in Kinnaur the data also suggest that the girls are also desired in the family, particularly by the women. It is perhaps due to the fact that women in the male dominated world like to find someone close to them. In the contemporary times, it is the daughter who provides, social, emotional and even economic security to the mother.

In fact, a good number of respondents favouring a son and a daughter in the family, besides being functional for maintaining a healthy sex-ratio, is indicative of the changing attitude of people towards sex preferences in Kinnaur. It is also desirable to mention here that the increasing mobility of the sons, their movement to other places and even getting married with the non-Kinnaura women may be one reason for this change. What way these factors contribute to this change in fertility behaviour is difficult to say. However, one of the implications of such a reasoning is that it requires further explorations into the intensity of change in the sex preferences, causes and conditions underlying changing sex preferences in Kinnaur.

The social structure with its changing institutions (i.e., marriage practices and nuclearisation of family) does not specify any ideal size of the family. The number of desired children varies from family to family. The ideal size of the family proposed by the individuals is significantly related with the actual number of children which people have. The variations in the desired number of children across different strata of people ranges between minimum two to maximum of four to six. The number of people desiring four or more children, like any other set of population, is limited and exist more as exceptions. It is also interesting to note that over the years, particularly after 1951 the population of Kinnaur has been increasing, but the size of the family has certainly receded. This is largely due to better women and child health.

In the context of family welfare programmes and their implementation, the response of the people in Himachal Pradesh as a whole is noted to be quite encouraging. The findings of the National Family Health Survey conducted in 1992, makes it quite explicit. In Kinnaur district, the data on the achievement of targets in implementation of various family planning devices reveal popularity of permanent methods, and that too among the women. Although the women are central to sexual reproduction, but some questions also arise: Why do more women than men go for tubectomy ? Is it due to patriarchal nature of the society ? Are there some other social structural reasons ?

It may be noted that the reasons, by and large, rest in the social structure itself. The role of patriarchy is also instrumental as it does not expect the man to lose his reproductive potentials. Second, there are certain fears associated with vasectomy. One of the main fears is becoming impotent. The other factors are sources of knowledge and motivation. The lady health workers get in touch with women more than their contact with men. It is the woman who is pressed more for tubectomy. The third reason perhaps states that from fertility point of view it is safe to get the wife sterilised.

Besides the use of permanent methods, the Kinnauras also make use of traditional as well as modern temporary methods. Among the traditional, the spacing method is most popular. It is also found that Kinnaur being a patriarchal society, the decision with regard to use of methods and who to use is taken by the males. The females are only to carry out the decision--willingly or unwillingly. The women, however, feel good about the use of family planning methods as it helps them avoid unwanted pregnancy, keep them away from the undue fear of pregnancy and enable them to have safe sex, and also help in avoiding contraction of any sexually transmitted diseases. Apart from making use of the family planning methods themselves, the women also convince their friends and relations to practice family planning for better personal and family health. In other words, it is the health consciousness which also makes the Kinnauras to resort to the use of family planning methods.

The use of family planning devices do have a positive impact on the fertility behaviour of women. But the use of various devices is influenced by a number of social structural factors. In turn, the fertility variations are influenced by different elements of social structure. Since the social structure expresses itself through its different elements, these elements also directly influence human behaviour, including the fertility behaviour. In Kinnaur too, social structural elements have been empirically found to influence human fertility.

In the social structure of Kinnaur caste constitutes one of the important factors of status determination. This factor is also found quite decisive in the determination of fertility differences between the high castes and the scheduled castes. According to the traditional basis of caste differentiation the scheduled castes are uneducated and poor in relation to the high castes. It is their poor conditions of living which determine their health status. Since the poor tend to have relatively higher mortality rate, the fertility tends to be high among them. Mahadevan (1979: 40-41) refers to the similar trends observed in the case of Gounders, Harijans and others. The Harijans tend to have higher fertility with corresponding higher crude death rates, infant and child mortality rates. The situation seems to persist in the same manner in Kinnaur today. The findings suggest that it is not caste per say which matters. It is the socio-economic and vital statistics of the caste concerned which causes significant variations in fertility.

The fertility is also associated with the awareness and knowledge about the family planning devices. The educational status of the person concerned is quite crucial in this regard. The study also indicates that the educational differences are also very crucial in the determination of fertility differences. It is imperative to mention that in Kinnaur women with higher education have less number of children than the women with less education. Similarly, the education of the husband is found to have critical linkages with the fertility behaviour. In the early 1970s, in the Indian context, it was stated that the impact of education in depressing fertility was visible only in the higher education categories, i.e., beyond the high school level (Aiyappan, in an introduction to Mahadevan's work, 1979: xxv). The lowering of the fertility was attributed to the modernising attitudes. This is no doubt true that the higher education by way of affecting occupational and social mobility induces attitudinal change which also has its impact on the number of children a family prefers to have. However, in Kinnaur it is found that fertility variations are visible even within the lower educational levels. It is not the education alone which makes a difference. The difference in the situation of then and now is also conditioned by the nature and intensity of family welfare measures, influence of mass media and many other such factors. In order to understand the impact of education and other intervening variables, it is desirable to initiate further studies on these aspects in Kinnaur.

The occupational status, the nature of occupation and the sector of employment also influence fertility differentials. The occupations which are quite strenuous and provide more chances of social and physical mobility tend to induce low fertility than the occupations which may be strenuous but do not have chances of social and physical mobility. In the rural setting, the occupational diversification among the women is very little. It, therefore, makes it difficult to say anything conclusive in this regard. However, the men have somewhat more chances of mobility and therefore, the nature and type of their occupation is more decisive than that of women. The analysis in this study also indicated association of differences between husband's occupational and fertility differences. It is important to mention that in Kinnaur neither the men have very well-diversified occupations nor the women. In the given situation of low occupational variations and almost nil social and occupational mobility the analysis remain inconclusive. But such a situation is not peculiar to Kinnaur alone but also have been found to exist even in a developed country like the United States of America. Boyd (1973) seems quite appropriate when he says that generalisation is not possible as it is the specific societal conditions in which the social mobility and reproduction take place.

The household income is one of the factors which creates class differences between different sets of population. The class differences constituted an important measure of fertility differentials. Freedman (1963), way back in the early 1960s made distinctions between the fertility among the poor and the rich families. Accordingly, the poor tended to have larger families than the rich classes. However, later studies tended to show, especially in the context of developed nations that income variations no longer remain important due to the shrinking differences between the middle and the upper classes. Although, in the context of Kinnaur today, the income differentials are not very large, and also show unequal distribution of the subjects studied, yet the data on income prove to be an important measure of association of differences between household income and fertility. The inverse relationship between income and fertility, even in the given low variations in the former, is suggestive of the influences which the income factor has on the fertility behaviour in Kinnaur. However, to be more authentic, a study with a larger and well-stratified sample may throw more light on the nature of this relationship.

The foregoing discussion, although at many points remains

inconclusive, throw considerable light on the relationship between social structure and fertility behaviour. The present study, a modest attempt restricted in analysis and contents, provides a base for much needed detailed and in-depth analysis in the field of tribal demography. It is, therefore, suggested that a study of local concepts related with fertility behaviour can provide more and in-depth insights.

Bibliography

Agarwala, S.N. (1967), *Age at Marriage in India*, Bombay: Kitab Mahal Private Limited.

Aiyappan, A. and K. Mahadevan (1990), *Ecology, Economy, Matrimony and Fertility of Kurichiyas*, Delhi: B.R. Publishing Corporation.

Babbie, Earl (1992), *The Practice of Social Research*, Belmont, California: Wadsworth Publishing Company.

Basu, Alka Malwade (1992), *Culture, Status of Women and Demographic Behaviour*, Oxford: Clarendon Press.

Bhatti, J.P. and others (1995), *Himachal Pradesh: National Family Health Survey 1992*, Shimla: Population Research Centre, (PRC) Himachal Pradesh University and Bombay: International Institute for Population Sciences (IIPS).

Blake, Judith (1961), *Family Structure in Jamaica: The Social Context of Reproduction*, Glencoe: The Free Press of Glencoe.

Bose, Ashish (1988), *From Population to People*, Delhi: B.R. Publishing House.

Bongaarts, John (1978), "A Framework of Analysing the Proximate Determinants of Fertility", *Population and Development Review*, Vol.4, No. 1, pp. 105-132.

Boyd, Monica (1973), "Occupational Mobility and Fertility in Metropolitan Latin America", *Demography*, Vol. 10, pp. 1-17.

Bruce, Judith (1991), *La qualite des services: un plus. Vie et Sante*, No. 6, pp. 10-12. (Discussed in The Annual Report of Population Council, New York, 1991).

Bumpass, L. (1969), "Age at Marriage as a Variable in Socio-economic Differentials in Fertility", *Demography*, Vol. 6, pp. 45-54.

Busfield, Joan (1991), "Age at Marriage and Family Size: Social-Causation and Social Selection Hypothesis", *Journal of Biosciences*, Vol. 4, pp. 117-134.

Caldwell, John C., P.H. Reddy and Pat Caldwell (1992), "The Causes of Demographic Change in Rural South India", *Population and Development Review*. Vol. 8, No. 4 (December). pp. 689-727.

Census of India (1991), *Himachal Pradesh*. Shimla: Government of India.

Chib, S.S. (1984), *Kinnauras of Trans-Himalayas*. Delhi.

Clifford, W.D. (1971), "Modern and Traditional Value Orientations and Fertility Behaviour: A Social Demographic Study", *Demography*, Vol. 8, pp. 37-48.

Coser, Lewis and B. Rosenberg (1976), *Sociological Theories: A Book of Readings*, Macmillan.

D'Souza, Victor S. (1983), *Economic Development and Population Growth*. Chandigarh: Population Research Centre, Punjab University (Unpublished).

Dandekar, Kumudini (1963), "Analysis of Birth Intervals of a Set of Indian Women", *Eugenics Quarterly*, Vol. 10 (2), pp. 73-78.

Devi Lalitha, V. (1982), *Status and Employment in India*, Delhi: B.R. Publishing Corporation.

Davis, Kingsley and Judith Blake (1968), "Social Structure and Fertility: An Analytic Framework", in Charles B. Nam (ed.) *Population and Society*, Boston: Houghton Mifflin Company, pp.196-215.

Davis, Kingsley and Wilbert E. Moore (1969), "Some Principles of Stratification", in R. Bendix et al., (eds.) *Class, Status and Party*.

Dixon, Ruth B. (1982), "Women in Agriculture: Counting the Labour Force in Developing Countries", *Population and Development Review*, Vol. 8, No.3, pp.539-66.

Driver, E.D. (1963), *Differential Fertility in Central India*, Princeton: Princeton University Press.

Easterlin, Richard A. and Eileen M. Crimmins (1982), *An Exploratory Analysis of the "Synthesis Framework" of Fertility Determination and World Fertility Survey Data,* World Fertility Survey Data Reports, No. 40, Voorburg, The Netherlands: International Statistical Institute.

Engels, F. (1948), *The Origin of Family, Private Property and the State*, Moscow: Progress Publishers.

Ford Foundation (1991), *Reproductive Health: Strategy for the 1990s.* New York.

Freedman, R.C., P.L. Whelpton and A.A. Campbell (1959), *Family Planning, Sterility and Population Growth*, New York: McGraw-Hill.

Giddens, Anthony (1995), *Sociology*, Cambridge: Polity Press.

Goldberg, D. (1959), "The Fertility of Two Generations", *Population Studies,* Vol. XII, pp. 214-222.

Goldberg, D. (1967), "Some Observations on Recent Changes in American Fertility Based on Sample Survey Data", *Eugenics Quarterly,* Vol. 14 (4), pp. 255-264.

Goldstein, Sidney (1972), "The Influence of Labour Force Participation and Education on Fertility in Thailand", *Population Studies* (London), Vol. 26, No. 3, pp. 419-436.

Goode, J.W. (1963), *World Revolution and Family Patterns*, New York: The Free Press.

Govindaswamy, Pavalavalli and Julie DaVanzo (1992), "Ethnicity and Fertility Differentials in Peninsular Malaysia: Do Policies Matter"? *Population and Development Review*, Vol. 18, No. 2, June. pp. 243-267.

Hoem, Jan M. (1990), "Social Policy and Recent Fertility Change in Sweden", *Population and Development Review*, Vol.16, No. 4, December. pp.735-748.

Hollingshed, A.B. and F.C. Redlich (1958), *Social Class and Mental Illness: A Community Study*, New York: Wiley.

Homans, G.C. (1950), *The Human Groups*, Harcourt Brace.

Jain, A.K. (1985), "The Impact of Development and Population Policies in India", *Studies in Family Planning*, Vol. 11, No.3 (September), pp.457-481.

Jain, Anuradh and Praveen Visaria (eds.) (1988), *Infant Mortality in India: Differentials and Determinants*, New Delhi: Sage Publications.

Jan, S.P. (1964), *Indian Fertility: Trends and Patterns*, New York: World Population Council.

Johnson, G.Z. (1960), *Differential Fertility in Europe: Demographic and Economic Change in Developed Countries*, Princeton: Princeton University Press.

Johnson, Harry M. (1983), *Sociology: A Systematic Introduction*, New Delhi: Allied Publishers Pvt. Limited.

Kane, P.V. (1941), *History of Dharamshastra*, Poona: Bhandarkar Oriental Research Institute, Vol. II, Part 1.

Kapadia, K.M. (1966), *Marriage and Family in India*, Madras: Oxford University Press.

Kazi, Shanaz and Zeba A. Sathar (1986), "Productive and Reproductive Choices: Report of a Pilot Survey of Urban Working Women in Karachi", *Pakistan Development Review*, Vol. 25, No. 4, pp. 593-608.

Kim, Y. (1965), "Age at Marriage and the Trends of Fertility in Korea", in Proceedings of the World Population Conference, pp. 145-148.

Kim, Y. (1965), "Age Patterns of Marriage and Rural-Urban Fertility. Differentials in Korea", pp. 371-37 (Unpublished Ph.D. Thesis, The Australian National University (referred in WPC 1965).

Kinsey, A.C. (1953), *Sexual Behaviour in the Human Female*, Saunders.

Kirk, D. (1968), "Factors Affecting Moslem Nationality", in Nam B. Charls (ed.) *Population and Society*, pp. 230-243.

Kiser, C.V. and P.K. Whelpton (1953), "Resume of the Indianapolis Study of Social and Psychological Factors Affecting Fertility", *Population Studies*, Vol. 7, No. 2, pp. 95-110.

Kupinsky, Stanley (1977), "The Fertility of Working Women in the United States: Historical Trends and Theoretical Perspectives", in

Stanley Kupinsky (ed.) *The Fertility of Working Women: A Synthesis of International Research*, New York: Praeger, pp. 188- 249.

Leacock, Eleanor Burke (1981), *Myths of Mail Dominance*, New York: Monthly Review Press.

Levi-Strauss (1974), "The family" in Harry Shapiro (ed.) *Man, Culture and Society*, London: Oxford University Press.

Linton, R. (1936), *The Study of Man: An Introduction*, in Lewis Coser and B. Rosenberg (eds.) *Sociological Theories: A Book of Readings*.

Llyod, Cynthia B. (1991), "The Contribution of the World Fertility Surveys to an Understanding of the Relationship between Women's Work and Fertility", *Studies in Family Planning*. Vol. 22, No. 3, pp. 144-61.

Lorimer, Frank et al., (1972), *Culture and Human Fertility*, Paris: UNESCO.

Mahadevan, K. (1979), *Sociology of Fertility Determinants of Fertility Differentials in South India*, New Delhi: Sterling Publishers Pvt. Ltd.

Mahadevan, K. and M. Sumangala (1987), *Social Development, Cultural Change and Fertility Decline*, New Delhi: Sage Publications.

Maine, Henry (1961), *Ancient Law*, Harmondsworth: Penguin.

Malhotra, Anju, Reeve Vinneman and Sunita Kishor (1985), "Fertility, Patriarchy and Development in India", *Population and Development Review*, Vol. 21, No. 2, June, pp. 281-306.

Marx, Karl (1963), "Economic and Philosophical Manuscripts", in T.B. Bottomore (ed.) *Marx: Early Writings*, Harmondsworth: Penguin.

McNicoll, Geoffrey (1991), "Review of Myron Weiner, The Child and the State in India: Child Labour and Education Policy in Comparative Perspective", *Population and Development Review*, Vol. 17, No. 3, pp. 531-534.

Mehta, Shalina (1998), "Rockets, Rackets and Targets: Demographic Trends in the Past and Future in India", in Keshav C. Kaistha and Satish K. Sharma (eds.) *Population, Spatial Mobility and Environment: Issues and Challenges for Sustainable Development*, New Delhi: Anamika Publisher.

Mencher, Joan P. (1980), "The Lessons and Non-lessons of Kerala: Agricultural Labourer and Poverty", *Economic and Political Weekly*. Vol. 15, Nos. 41-43, pp. 1781-1802.

Mencher, Joan P. and Anne Okongwu (eds.) (1993), *Where Did All the Men Go? Female Headed/ Female Supported Households in Cross-Cultural Perspective*, Boulder: Westview Press.

Merton, R.K. (1957), *Social Theory and Social Structure: Towards the Codification of Theory and Research*, Free Press.

Mhloyi, Marvellous (1991), "Fertility Transition in Zimbabwe" discussed in Shireen J. Jejeebhoy (1996), "Women's Education, Fertility and Proximate Determinants of Fertility", (United Nations 1996, *Population and Women*).

Mitchel, J.C. (1971), "Cultural Explanations of Fertility Differences", *Journal of Biosocial Science*, Vol. 3.

Mueller, Eva (1975), "The Impact of Agriculture Change on Demographic Development in the Third World", in Leon Tabah (ed.) *Population Growth and Economic Development in the Third World.*

Mueller, Eva (1976), "The Economic Value of Children in Peasant Agriculture", in Ronald Ridker (ed.) *Population and Development*, Baltimore, Maryland: The Johns Hopkins University Press.

Mueller, Eva (1982), "The Allocation of Women's Time and its Relation to Fertility", in Richard Anker et al., (eds.) *Women's Roles and Population Trends in the Third World*, Geneva: ILO, pp. 55-86.

Mukherjee, S.B. (1961), *Studies on Fertility Rates in Calcutta*, Calcutta: Bookland Private Ltd.

Murdock, G.P. (1949), *Social Structure*, London: Macmillan.

Nag, Moni (1981), "Impact of Social Development and Economic Development on Mortality: A Comparative Study of Kerala and West Bengal", Working Paper 78, New York Population Council.

Nag, Moni (1983), "The Equity Fertility Hypothesis as an Explanation of the Fertility Differential Between Kerala and West Bengal", Working Paper 96, New York: Population Council.

Negi, T.S. (1973), *Gazetteer of Kinnaur*, Shimla: Government of Himachal Pradesh.

Oni, Gbolahan A. (1985), "Effects of Women's Education on Post-Partum Practices and Fertility in Urban Nigeria", *Studies in Family Planning*, Vol. 16, No. 6, pp. 321-331.

PACR (1991), *The Annual Report of Population Council*, New York: Population Council.

Patel, Tulsi (1990), "Modernization and Changing Fertility Behaviour in a Rajasthan Village", *Sociological Bulletin*, Vol. 39, Nos. 1 and 2, pp. 53-74.

Phillips, J.F. and J.A. Ross (1992), *Family Planning Programmes and Fertility*, Oxford: Clarendon Press.

Premi, Mahendra K. (1998), "Population Policies and Programmers: Issues for 1990s and Beyond", in Keshav, C. Kaistha and Satish K. Sharma (eds.) *Population, Spatial Mobility and Environment: Issues and Challenges for Sustainable Development*, New Delhi: Anamika Publisher.

Radcliffe-Brown, A.R., *Structure and Function in Primitive Society*, Oxford: Oxford University Press.

Rainwater, L. (1965), *Family Design: Marital Sexuality, Family Size and Contraception*, Chicago: Aldine Publishing Company.

Ratcliffe, John (1978), "Social Justice and Demographic Transition: Lessons from India's Kerala State", *International Journal of Health Services*, Vol. 8, No. 1, pp. 123-144.

Reiter, Rayna R. (ed.) (1975), *Toward an Anthropology of Women*, New York: Monthly Review Press.

Rele, et al. (1972), "Residence Background and Fertility in Greater Bombay", *Population Studies*, Vol. 28, pp. 299-308.

Ritchey, and E.S. Stokes (1972), "Residence Background, Migration and Fertility", *Demography*, Vol. 9, pp. 217-230.

Rosaldo, Michelle and Loiuse Lamphere (eds.) (1974), *Women, Culture and Society*, Stanford: Stanford University Press.

Roy Burman, B.K. (1994), "Tribal Population: Interface of Historical Ecology and Political Economy", in Mrinal Miri (ed.) *Continuity and Change in Tribal Society*, Shimla: Indian Institute of Advanced Studies.

Sanday, Peggy R. (1974), "Female Status in Public Domain", in Michelle Rosaldo and Louise Lamphere (eds.), *Women Culture and Society*, Stanford: University Press.

Sathar, Zeba A. et al., (1988), "Women's Status and Fertility Change in Pakistan", *Population and Development Review*, Vol. 14, No. 3, pp. 413-432.

Sathar, Zeba A. et al., (1990), "Women, Work and Family Planning in Karachi", *International Family Planning Perspectives*, New York, Vol. 16, No. 2, pp. 66-69.

Sharma, A.K. (1987), *Fertility and Family Planning in Rural Areas*, New Delhi: Mittal Publications.

Sharma, Ravi K. et al., (1990), "A Comparative Analysis of Trends and Differentials in Breastfeeding: Findings from DHS Survey", (discussed in United Nations Secretariat (1996), *Population and Women.*

Sharma, Roshan Lal (1995), "Social Development, Social Mobility and Fertility Behaviour: A Study of Rural Himachal Pradesh", (Unpublished Ph. D. Thesis), Department of Sociology, Himachal Pradesh University, Shimla.

Sharma, Satish K. (1997), *Population, Urbanization and Environment*, A Report submitted to State Council of Science Technology and Environment, Government of Himachal Pradesh, Shimla (Unpublished).

Sharma, Urusula (1983), *Women's Work and Property in North-West India*, London: Tavistock Publications.

Singh, Susheela et al., (1988), "The Proximate Determinants of Fertility: Sub-national Variations", *Population Studies* (London), Vol. 39, No. 1, pp. 113-135.

Sinha, U.P. (1994), "The Demographic Situation of Tribals in India", in Mrinal Miri (ed.) *Continuity and Change in Tribal Society*, Shimla: Indian Institute of Advanced Studies.

Sivard, R.L. (1985), *Women: A World Survey*, Washington, D.C.: World Priorities.

Smelser, Neil J. (1993), *An Introduction to Sociology*, New Delhi: Prentice Hall of India Pvt. Ltd.

Spengler, J.J. and Duncan D.D. (1966), *Population Theory and Policy*, Glencoe, Illinois: The Free Press.

Srinivasan, R. (1988), "Impact of Population on Selected Social and Economic Sector", *Economic and Political Weekly*, September. pp. 1933-1975.

Stycos, J.M. and R.H. Weller (1967), "Female Working Roles and Fertility", *Demography*, 4 (1), pp 210-217.

Stycos, J.M. (1968), "Social Class and Differential Fertility in Peru", in Charls B. Nam (ed.) *Population and Society.*

Sumner, W.G. (1906), *Folkways: A Study of the Sociological Importance of Usages, Manners, Customs, Mores and Morals*, Ginn.

Tabah, Leon (ed.) (1975), *Population Growth and Economic Development in the Third World*, Belgium: IUSSP (Ardina Editions).

Thakur, Savita and Dalip S. Thakur (1995), "Female Work Participation and Their Decision Making Power: A Micro Level Study in Himachal Pradesh", *PSE Economic Analyst*, Vol. XVI, No. 1& 2, pp. 61-69.

Tumin, Melvin M. (1987), *Social Stratification: The Forms and Functions of Inequality,* New Delhi: Prentice Hall of India Pvt. Ltd.

United Nations (1961), *The Mysore Population Study*, Report of a Field Survey carried out in selected area of Mysore State, India, pp. 88-266.

United Nations (1985), "Women's Employment and Fertility: A Comparative Analysis of World Fertility Survey Results for 38 Developing Countries", *Population Studies*, No. 96.

United Nations (1985), *Achievements of the United Nations Decade for Women: Equality, Development and Peace*, Nairobi: Kenya (15-26 July, 1985).

United Nations (1993), *Women's Education and Fertility Behaviour: A Case Study of Rural Maharashtra, India*, New York: Department of Economic and Social Information and Policy analysis.

United Nations (1995), *Living Arrangements of Women and their Children in Developing Countries: A Demographic Profile*, New York: Department for Economic and Social Information and Policy Analysis (population division).

United Nations (1993), *Women's Status and Fertility in Pakistan: Recent Evidence*, New York: Department for Economic and Social Information and Policy Analysis.

United Nations (1994), *International Conference on Population*, New York: Department of Economic and Social Information and Policy Analysis.

United Nations (1996), *Population and Women*, New York: Department of Economic and Social Information and Policy Analysis.

Warner, W.L. Lloyd and Lunt P.S. (1941), *The Social Life of a Modern Community*, Yale: Yale University Press.

Warner, W.L. Lloyd and Lunt P.S. (1947), *The Status System of a Modern Community*, New Haven, Conn: Yale University Press.

Weber, Max (1974), "Class, Status and Party", in Joseph Lopreato and S. Lewis (eds.) *Social Stratification: A Reader*, New York: Harper and Row.

Weber, Max (1978), *Economy and Society: An Outline of Interpretive Sociology*, (Vol. 2) Berkeley: University of California Press.

Weller, R. and D.F. Sly (1969), "Modernization and Demographic Change: A World View", *Rural Sociology*, Vol. 34 (3): pp 313-326.

Wyon, J.B. and J.E. Gorden (1971), *The Khanna Study: Population Problems in the Rural Punjab*, Cambridge: Harvard University Press.

Zacharia, K.C. (1983), "Land Reforms and Fertility Decline in Kerala", *Demography India*, Vol. XIII, No. 2, pp. 173-178.

Zeidenstein, George (1992), President's Message: In Pursuit of Safe Motherhood, in *The Population Council Annual Report 1991*. New York.

Index